POWERSHELL AND SQL CLIENT

Working with the Datatable

Richard Thomas Edwards

CONTENTS

WHY IS THE CODE BROKEN INTO SECTIONS?

This book is really condensed

THIS BOOK IS REALL A HUGE BOOK! It just doesn't look that way if you're looking at just the length of it. For example, if you were to eliminate the stylesheets, there are approximately 68 pages before I added one – just one – example of a complete code example. In-other-words, 6 pages of one code example is almost 10 percent of this book. Imagine what 5760 would look like at just 5 pages each! This book would wind up being 28800 pages in length.

Yet, it is, indeed, all here!

```
$cnstr = """
$strQuery = """

$cn = new-object System.Data.SqlClient.SqlConnection
$cn.ConnectionString = $cnstr
$cn.Open()

$cmd = new-object System.Data.SqlClient.SqlCommand
$cmd.Connection = $cn
$cmd.CommandType = 1
$cmd.CommandText = strQuery
$cmd.ExecuteNonquery()
```

```
$da = new-object System.Data.SqlClient.SqlDataAdapter($cmd)

$dt = new-object System.Data.Datatable
$da.Fill($dt)

$ws = new-object -com WScript.Shell
$fso = new-object -com Scripting.FileSystemObject
$txtstream = $fso.OpenTextFile($ws.CurrentDirectory + "\Products.html", 1,
$true, -2)
$txtstream.WriteLine("<html>")
$txtstream.WriteLine("<head>")
$txtstream.WriteLine("<title>Products</title>")
$txtstream.WriteLine("<style type='text/css'>")
$txtstream.WriteLine("body")
$txtstream.WriteLine("{")
$txtstream.WriteLine("    PADDING-RIGHT: 0px;")
$txtstream.WriteLine("    PADDING-LEFT: 0px;")
$txtstream.WriteLine("    PADDING-BOTTOM: 0px;")
$txtstream.WriteLine("    MARGIN: 0px;")
$txtstream.WriteLine("    COLOR: #333;")
$txtstream.WriteLine("    PADDING-TOP: 0px;")
$txtstream.WriteLine("    FONT-FAMILY: verdana, arial, helvetica, sans-serif;")
$txtstream.WriteLine("}")
$txtstream.WriteLine("table")
$txtstream.WriteLine("{")
$txtstream.WriteLine("    BORDER-RIGHT: #999999 1px solid;")
$txtstream.WriteLine("    PADDING-RIGHT: 1px;")
$txtstream.WriteLine("    PADDING-LEFT: 1px;")
$txtstream.WriteLine("    PADDING-BOTTOM: 1px;")
$txtstream.WriteLine("    LINE-HEIGHT: 8px;")
$txtstream.WriteLine("    PADDING-TOP: 1px;")
$txtstream.WriteLine("    BORDER-BOTTOM: #999 1px solid;")
$txtstream.WriteLine("    BACKGROUND-COLOR: #eeeeee;")
$txtstream.WriteLine("
filter:progid:DXImageTransform.Microsoft.Shadow(color='silver', Direction=135,
Strength=16)")
$txtstream.WriteLine("}")
$txtstream.WriteLine("th")
$txtstream.WriteLine("{")
$txtstream.WriteLine("    BORDER-RIGHT: #999999 3px solid;")
$txtstream.WriteLine("    PADDING-RIGHT: 6px;")
$txtstream.WriteLine("    PADDING-LEFT: 6px;")
$txtstream.WriteLine("    FONT-WEIGHT: Bold;")
$txtstream.WriteLine("    FONT-SIZE: 14px;")
$txtstream.WriteLine("    PADDING-BOTTOM: 6px;")
$txtstream.WriteLine("    COLOR: darkred;")
$txtstream.WriteLine("    LINE-HEIGHT: 14px;")
$txtstream.WriteLine("    PADDING-TOP: 6px;")
$txtstream.WriteLine("    BORDER-BOTTOM: #999 1px solid;")
$txtstream.WriteLine("    BACKGROUND-COLOR: #eeeeee;")
```

```
$txtstream.WriteLine("   FONT-FAMILY: font-family: Cambria, serif;")
$txtstream.WriteLine("   FONT-SIZE: 12px;")
$txtstream.WriteLine("   text-align: left;")
$txtstream.WriteLine("   white-Space: nowrap='nowrap';")
$txtstream.WriteLine("}")
$txtstream.WriteLine(".th")
$txtstream.WriteLine("{")
$txtstream.WriteLine("   BORDER-RIGHT: #999999 2px solid;")
$txtstream.WriteLine("   PADDING-RIGHT: 6px;")
$txtstream.WriteLine("   PADDING-LEFT: 6px;")
$txtstream.WriteLine("   FONT-WEIGHT: Bold;")
$txtstream.WriteLine("   PADDING-BOTTOM: 6px;")
$txtstream.WriteLine("   COLOR: black;")
$txtstream.WriteLine("   PADDING-TOP: 6px;")
$txtstream.WriteLine("   BORDER-BOTTOM: #999 2px solid;")
$txtstream.WriteLine("   BACKGROUND-COLOR: #eeeeee;")
$txtstream.WriteLine("   FONT-FAMILY: font-family: Cambria, serif;")
$txtstream.WriteLine("   FONT-SIZE: 10px;")
$txtstream.WriteLine("   text-align: right;")
$txtstream.WriteLine("   white-Space: nowrap='nowrap';")
$txtstream.WriteLine("}")
$txtstream.WriteLine("td")
$txtstream.WriteLine("{")
$txtstream.WriteLine("   BORDER-RIGHT: #999999 3px solid;")
$txtstream.WriteLine("   PADDING-RIGHT: 6px;")
$txtstream.WriteLine("   PADDING-LEFT: 6px;")
$txtstream.WriteLine("   FONT-WEIGHT: Normal;")
$txtstream.WriteLine("   PADDING-BOTTOM: 6px;")
$txtstream.WriteLine("   COLOR: navy;")
$txtstream.WriteLine("   LINE-HEIGHT: 14px;")
$txtstream.WriteLine("   PADDING-TOP: 6px;")
$txtstream.WriteLine("   BORDER-BOTTOM: #999 1px solid;")
$txtstream.WriteLine("   BACKGROUND-COLOR: #eeeeee;")
$txtstream.WriteLine("   FONT-FAMILY: font-family: Cambria, serif;")
$txtstream.WriteLine("   FONT-SIZE: 12px;")
$txtstream.WriteLine("   text-align: left;")
$txtstream.WriteLine("   white-Space: nowrap='nowrap';")
$txtstream.WriteLine("}")
$txtstream.WriteLine("div")
$txtstream.WriteLine("{")
$txtstream.WriteLine("   BORDER-RIGHT: #999999 3px solid;")
$txtstream.WriteLine("   PADDING-RIGHT: 6px;")
$txtstream.WriteLine("   PADDING-LEFT: 6px;")
$txtstream.WriteLine("   FONT-WEIGHT: Normal;")
$txtstream.WriteLine("   PADDING-BOTTOM: 6px;")
$txtstream.WriteLine("   COLOR: white;")
$txtstream.WriteLine("   PADDING-TOP: 6px;")
$txtstream.WriteLine("   BORDER-BOTTOM: #999 1px solid;")
$txtstream.WriteLine("   BACKGROUND-COLOR: navy;")
$txtstream.WriteLine("   FONT-FAMILY: font-family: Cambria, serif;")
```

```
$txtstream.WriteLine("    FONT-SIZE: 10px;")
$txtstream.WriteLine("    text-align: left;")
$txtstream.WriteLine("    white-Space: nowrap='nowrap';")
$txtstream.WriteLine("}")
$txtstream.WriteLine("span")
$txtstream.WriteLine("{")
$txtstream.WriteLine("    BORDER-RIGHT: #999999 3px solid;")
$txtstream.WriteLine("    PADDING-RIGHT: 3px;")
$txtstream.WriteLine("    PADDING-LEFT: 3px;")
$txtstream.WriteLine("    FONT-WEIGHT: Normal;")
$txtstream.WriteLine("    PADDING-BOTTOM: 3px;")
$txtstream.WriteLine("    COLOR: white;")
$txtstream.WriteLine("    PADDING-TOP: 3px;")
$txtstream.WriteLine("    BORDER-BOTTOM: #999 1px solid;")
$txtstream.WriteLine("    BACKGROUND-COLOR: navy;")
$txtstream.WriteLine("    FONT-FAMILY: font-family: Cambria, serif;")
$txtstream.WriteLine("    FONT SIZE: 10px;")
$txtstream.WriteLine("    text-align: left;")
$txtstream.WriteLine("    white-Space: nowrap='nowrap';")
$txtstream.WriteLine("    display: inline-block;")
$txtstream.WriteLine("    width: 100%;")
$txtstream.WriteLine("}")
$txtstream.WriteLine("textarea")
$txtstream.WriteLine("{")
$txtstream.WriteLine("    BORDER-RIGHT: #999999 3px solid;")
$txtstream.WriteLine("    PADDING-RIGHT: 3px;")
$txtstream.WriteLine("    PADDING-LEFT: 3px;")
$txtstream.WriteLine("    FONT-WEIGHT: Normal;")
$txtstream.WriteLine("    PADDING-BOTTOM: 3px;")
$txtstream.WriteLine("    COLOR: white;")
$txtstream.WriteLine("    PADDING-TOP: 3px;")
$txtstream.WriteLine("    BORDER-BOTTOM: #999 1px solid;")
$txtstream.WriteLine("    BACKGROUND-COLOR: navy;")
$txtstream.WriteLine("    FONT-FAMILY: font-family: Cambria, serif;")
$txtstream.WriteLine("    FONT-SIZE: 10px;")
$txtstream.WriteLine("    text-align: left;")
$txtstream.WriteLine("    white-Space: nowrap='nowrap';")
$txtstream.WriteLine("    width: 100%;")
$txtstream.WriteLine("}")
$txtstream.WriteLine("select")
$txtstream.WriteLine("{")
$txtstream.WriteLine("    BORDER-RIGHT: #999999 3px solid;")
$txtstream.WriteLine("    PADDING-RIGHT: 6px;")
$txtstream.WriteLine("    PADDING-LEFT: 6px;")
$txtstream.WriteLine("    FONT-WEIGHT: Normal;")
$txtstream.WriteLine("    PADDING-BOTTOM: 6px;")
$txtstream.WriteLine("    COLOR: white;")
$txtstream.WriteLine("    PADDING-TOP: 6px;")
$txtstream.WriteLine("    BORDER-BOTTOM: #999 1px solid;")
$txtstream.WriteLine("    BACKGROUND-COLOR: navy;")
```

```
$txtstream.WriteLine("    FONT-FAMILY: font-family: Cambria, serif;")
$txtstream.WriteLine("    FONT-SIZE: 10px;")
$txtstream.WriteLine("    text-align: left;")
$txtstream.WriteLine("    white-Space: nowrap='nowrap';")
$txtstream.WriteLine("    width: 100%;")
$txtstream.WriteLine("}")
$txtstream.WriteLine("input")
$txtstream.WriteLine("{")
$txtstream.WriteLine("    BORDER-RIGHT: #999999 3px solid;")
$txtstream.WriteLine("    PADDING-RIGHT: 3px;")
$txtstream.WriteLine("    PADDING-LEFT: 3px;")
$txtstream.WriteLine("    FONT-WEIGHT: Bold;")
$txtstream.WriteLine("    PADDING-BOTTOM: 3px;")
$txtstream.WriteLine("    COLOR: white;")
$txtstream.WriteLine("    PADDING-TOP: 3px;")
$txtstream.WriteLine("    BORDER-BOTTOM: #999 1px solid;")
$txtstream.WriteLine("    BACKGROUND-COLOR: navy;")
$txtstream.WriteLine("    FONT-FAMILY: font-family: Cambria, serif;")
$txtstream.WriteLine("    FONT-SIZE: 12px;")
$txtstream.WriteLine("    text-align: left;")
$txtstream.WriteLine("    display: table-cell;")
$txtstream.WriteLine("    white-Space: nowrap='nowrap';")
$txtstream.WriteLine("    width: 100%;")
$txtstream.WriteLine("}")
$txtstream.WriteLine("h1 {")
$txtstream.WriteLine("color: antiquewhite;")
$txtstream.WriteLine("text-shadow: 1px 1px 1px black;")
$txtstream.WriteLine("padding: 3px;")
$txtstream.WriteLine("text-align: center;")
$txtstream.WriteLine("box-shadow: inset 2px 2px 5px rgba(0,0,0,0.5), inset -2px
-2px 5px rgba(255,255,255,0.5);")
$txtstream.WriteLine("}")
$txtstream.WriteLine("</style>")
$txtstream.WriteLine("<body>")
$txtstream.WriteLine("<center>")
$txtstream.WriteLine("</br>")
$txtstream.WriteLine("</br>")
$txtstream.WriteLine("<table border=0 cellspacing=3 cellpadding=3>")
$txtstream.WriteLine("<tr>")
foreach($Col in  $dt.Columns)
{
    $txtstream.WriteLine("<th align='left' nowrap='nowrap'>" + $col.Caption +
"</th>")
}
$txtstream.WriteLine("</tr>")

foreach($dr in  $dt.Rows)
{
    $txtstream.WriteLine("<tr>")
    for each($col in  $dt.Columns)
```

```
        {
            $txtstream.WriteLine("<td  align='left' nowrap='true'><input type=text
value='" + $dr[$col.Caption].ToString() + "'></input></td>")
        }
        $txtstream.WriteLine("</tr>")
    }
    $txtstream.WriteLine("</table>")
    $txtstream.WriteLine("</body>")
    $txtstream.WriteLine("</html>")
    $txtstream.Close()
```

A LOT OF CODE TO COVER

Overview

THERE IS A LOT OF CODE TO COVER AND, HONESTLY, I HATE INTRODUCTIONS. So, let's make this short and sweet. We're using SQL CLIENT and the Datatable to create outputs that include ASP, ASPX, Delimited Text Files, Excel, HTA, HTML, XML, and XSL. There, I said it, I'm done. From the Sql Client coding perspective, use the following:

```
$cnstr = ""; 
$strQuery = ""
```

Connection, Command and DataAdapter

```
$cn = new-object System.Data.SqlClient.SqlConnection
$cn.ConnectionString = $cnstr
$cn.Open();

$cmd = new-object System.Data.SqlClient.SqlCommand
$cmd.Connection = $cn
$cmd.CommandType = 1
$cmd.CommandText = $strQuery
```

```
$cmd.ExecuteNonquery()

$da = new-object System.Data.SqlClient.SqlDataAdapter($cmd)

$dt = new-object System.Data.DataTable
$da.Fill($dt)
```

Connection and DataAdapter

```
$cn = new-object System.Data.SqlClient.SqlConnection
$cn.ConnectionString = $cnstr
$cn.Open()

$da = new-object System.Data.SqlClient.SqlDataAdapter($strQuery, $cn)

$dt = new-object System.Data.DataTable
$da.Fill($dt)
```

Command and DataAdapter

```
$cmd = new-object System.Data.SqlClient.SqlCommand
$cmd.Connection = new-object System.Data.SqlClient.SqlConnection
$cmd.Connection.ConnectionString = $cnstr
$cmd.Connection.Open()
$cmd.CommandType = 1
$cmd.CommandText = strQuery
$cmd.ExecuteNonQuery()

$da = new-object System.Data.SqlClient.SqlDataAdapter($cmd)

$dt = new-object System.Data.DataTable
$da.Fill($dt)
```

DataAdapter

```
$da = new-object System.Data.SqlClient.SqlDataAdapter($strQuery, $cnstr)

$dt = new-object System.Data.DataTable
$da.Fill($dt)
```

You are going to need to add one of the above ways to populate the dataadapter to the routines you plan on using.

ASP EXAMPLES

Let's do it!

B elow, are examples of using SQL CLIENT, the Datatable and ASP. And just in case you are wondering, I use none as meaning no additional tags between the <td></td>.

HORIZONTAL

```
$ws = new-object -com WScript.Shell
$fso = new-object -com Scripting.FileSystemObject
$txtstream = $fso.OpenTextFile($ws.CurrentDirectory + "\\Products.asp", 2,
$true, -2)
$txtstream.WriteLine("<html>")
$txtstream.WriteLine("<head>")
$txtstream.WriteLine("<title>Products</title>")
$txtstream.WriteLine("<body>")
```

For Reports:

```
$txtstream.WriteLine("<table border=0 cellspacing=3 cellpadding=3>")
```

For Tables:

```
$txtstream.WriteLine("<table border=1 cellspacing=3 cellpadding=3>")

$txtstream.WriteLine("<%")
$txtstream.WriteLine("Response.Write('<tr>' & vbcrlf)")
for each($col in $dt.Columns)
{
```

```
    $txtstream.WriteLine("Response.Write('<th align='left' nowrap='nowrap'>" +
$col.Caption + "</th>' & vbcrlf)")
    }
    $txtstream.WriteLine("Response.Write('</tr>' & vbcrlf)")
```

Additional Tags:

None

```
    foreach($dr in $dt.Rows)
    {
        $txtstream.WriteLine("Response.Write('<tr>' & vbcrlf)")
        for each($col in $dt.Columns)
        {
            $txtstream.WriteLine("Response.Write('<td align='left' nowrap='nowrap'>"
+ $dr[$col.Caption].ToString() + "</td>' & vbcrlf)")
        }
        $txtstream.WriteLine("Response.Write('</tr>' & vbcrlf)")
    }
```

Button

```
    foreach($dr in $dt.Rows)
    {
        $txtstream.WriteLine("Response.Write('<tr>' & vbcrlf)")
        for each($col in $dt.Columns)
        {
            $txtstream.WriteLine("Response.Write('<td align='left'
nowrap='true'><button style='width:100%;' value ='" + $dr[$col.Caption].ToString()
+ "'>" + $dr[$col.Caption].ToString() + "</button></td>' & vbcrlf)")
        }
        $txtstream.WriteLine("Response.Write('</tr>' & vbcrlf)")
    }
```

Combobox

```
    foreach($dr in $dt.Rows)
    {
        $txtstream.WriteLine("Response.Write('<tr>' & vbcrlf)")
        for each($col in $dt.Columns)
        {
            $txtstream.WriteLine("Response.Write('<td align='left'
nowrap='true'><select><option value = '" + $dr[$col.Caption].ToString() + "'>" +
$dr[$col.Caption].ToString() + "</option></select></td>' & vbcrlf)")
        }
        $txtstream.WriteLine("Response.Write('</tr>' & vbcrlf)")
    }
```

Div

```
foreach($dr in  $dt.Rows)
{
    $txtstream.WriteLine("Response.Write('<tr>' & vbcrlf)")
    for each($col in  $dt.Columns)
    {
        $txtstream.WriteLine("Response.Write('<td  align='left'
nowrap='true'><div>" + $dr[$col.Caption].ToString() + "</div></td>' & vbcrlf)")
    }
    $txtstream.WriteLine("Response.Write('</tr>' & vbcrlf)")
}
```

Link

```
foreach($dr in  $dt.Rows)
{
    $txtstream.WriteLine("Response.Write('<tr>' & vbcrlf)")
    for each($col in  $dt.Columns)
    {
        $txtstream.WriteLine("Response.Write('<td  align='left' nowrap='true'><a
href='" + $dr[$col.Caption].ToString() + "'>" + $dr[$col.Caption].ToString() +
"</a></td>' & vbcrlf)")
    }
    $txtstream.WriteLine("Response.Write('</tr>' & vbcrlf)")
}
```

Listbox

```
foreach($dr in  $dt.Rows)
{
    $txtstream.WriteLine("Response.Write('<tr>' & vbcrlf)")
    for each($col in  $dt.Columns)
    {
        $txtstream.WriteLine("Response.Write('<td  align='left'
nowrap='true'><select multiple><option value = '" + $dr[$col.Caption].ToString() +
"'>" + $dr[$col.Caption].ToString() + "</option></select></td>' & vbcrlf)")
    }
    $txtstream.WriteLine("Response.Write('</tr>' & vbcrlf)")
}
```

Span

```
foreach($dr in  $dt.Rows)
{
```

```
    $txtstream.WriteLine("Response.Write('<tr>' & vbcrlf)")
    for each($col in $dt.Columns)
    {
        $txtstream.WriteLine("Response.Write('<td align='left'
nowrap='true'><span>" + $dr[$col.Caption].ToString() + "</span></td>' & vbcrlf)")
    }
    $txtstream.WriteLine("Response.Write('</tr>' & vbcrlf)")
  }
```

Textarea

```
  foreach($dr in $dt.Rows)
  {
    $txtstream.WriteLine("Response.Write('<tr>' & vbcrlf)")
    for each($col in $dt.Columns)
    {
        $txtstream.WriteLine("Response.Write('<td align='left'
nowrap='true'><textarea>" + $dr[$col.Caption].ToString() + "</textarea></td>' &
vbcrlf)")
    }
    $txtstream.WriteLine("Response.Write('</tr>' & vbcrlf)")
  }
```
Textbox

```
  foreach($dr in $dt.Rows)
  {
    $txtstream.WriteLine("Response.Write('<tr>' & vbcrlf)")
    for each($col in $dt.Columns)
    {
        $txtstream.WriteLine("Response.Write('<td align='left'
nowrap='true'><input type=text value='" + $dr[$col.Caption].ToString() +
"'></input></td>' & vbcrlf)")
    }
    $txtstream.WriteLine("Response.Write('</tr>' & vbcrlf)")
  }
```

End Code

```
  $txtstream.WriteLine("%>")
  $txtstream.WriteLine("</table>")
  $txtstream.WriteLine("</body>")
  $txtstream.WriteLine("</html>")
  $txtstream.Close()
```

VERTICAL

```
$ws = new-object -com WScript.Shell
$fso = new-object -com Scripting.FileSystemObject
$txtstream = $fso.OpenTextFile($ws.CurrentDirectory + "\\Products.asp", 2,
$true, -2)
$txtstream.WriteLine("<html>")
$txtstream.WriteLine("<head>")
$txtstream.WriteLine("<title>Products</title>")
$txtstream.WriteLine("<body>")
$txtstream.WriteLine("<center>")
$txtstream.WriteLine("</br>")
$txtstream.WriteLine("</br>")
```

For Reports:

```
$txtstream.WriteLine("<table border=0 cellspacing=3 cellpadding=3>")
```

For Tables:

```
$txtstream.WriteLine("<table border=1 cellspacing=3 cellpadding=3>")

$txtstream.WriteLine("<%")
for each($col in $dt.Columns)
{
    $txtstream.WriteLine("Response.Write('<tr><th align='left'
nowrap='nowrap'>" + $col.Caption + "</th>' & vbcrlf)")
```

None

```
    foreach($dr in $dt.Rows)
    {
        $txtstream.WriteLine("Response.Write('<td align='left' nowrap='nowrap'>"
+ $dr[$col.Caption].ToString() + "</td>' & vbcrlf)")
    }
```

Additional Tags:

None

```
    foreach($dr in $dt.Rows)
    {
```

```
        $txtstream.WriteLine("Response.Write('<td align='left' nowrap='nowrap'>"
+ $dr[$col.Caption].ToString() + "</td>' & vbcrlf)")
    }
```

Button

```
    foreach($dr in  $dt.Rows)
    {
        $txtstream.WriteLine("Response.Write('<td  align='left'
nowrap='true'><button style='width:100%;' value ='" + $dr[$col.Caption].ToString()
+ "'>" + $dr[$col.Caption].ToString() + "</button></td>' & vbcrlf)")
    }
```

Combobox

```
    foreach($dr in  $dt.Rows)
    {
        $txtstream.WriteLine("Response.Write('<td  align='left'
nowrap='true'><select><option value = '" + $dr[$col.Caption].ToString() + "'>" +
$dr[$col.Caption].ToString() + "</option></select></td>' & vbcrlf)")
    }
```

Div

```
    foreach($dr in  $dt.Rows)
    {
        $txtstream.WriteLine("Response.Write('<td  align='left'
nowrap='true'><div>" + $dr[$col.Caption].ToString() + "</div></td>' & vbcrlf)")
    }
```

Link

```
    foreach($dr in  $dt.Rows)
    {
        $txtstream.WriteLine("Response.Write('<td  align='left' nowrap='true'><a
href='" + $dr[$col.Caption].ToString() + "'>" + $dr[$col.Caption].ToString() +
"</a></td>' & vbcrlf)")
    }
```

Listbox

```
    foreach($dr in  $dt.Rows)
    {
        $txtstream.WriteLine("Response.Write('<td  align='left'
nowrap='true'><select multiple><option value = '" + $dr[$col.Caption].ToString() +
"'>" + $dr[$col.Caption].ToString() + "</option></select></td>' & vbcrlf)")
```

```
        }
```
Span

```
        foreach($dr in $dt.Rows)
        {
            $txtstream.WriteLine("Response.Write('<td align='left'
nowrap='true'><span>" + $dr[$col.Caption].ToString() + "</span></td>' & vbcrlf)")
        }
```

Textarea

```
        foreach($dr in $dt.Rows)
        {
            $txtstream.WriteLine("Response.Write('<td align='left'
nowrap='true'><textarea>" + $dr[$col.Caption].ToString() + "</textarea></td>' &
vbcrlf)")
        }
```

Textbox

```
        foreach($dr in $dt.Rows)
        {
            $txtstream.WriteLine("Response.Write('<td align='left'
nowrap='true'><input type=text value='" + $dr[$col.Caption].ToString() +
'"></input></td>' & vbcrlf)")
        }
```

End Code

```
        $txtstream.WriteLine("Response.Write('</tr>' & vbcrlf)")
    }
    $txtstream.WriteLine("%>")
    $txtstream.WriteLine("</table>")
    $txtstream.WriteLine("</body>")
    $txtstream.WriteLine("</html>")
    $txtstream.Close()
```

ASPX EXAMPLES

Yes, you can!

Below, are examples of using SQL CLIENT, the Datatable and ASPX. And just in case you are wondering, I use none as meaning no additional tags between the <td></td>

HORIZONTAL

```
$ws = new-object -com WScript.Shell
$fso = new-object -com Scripting.FileSystemObject
$txtstream = $fso.OpenTextFile($ws.CurrentDirectory + "\\Products.asp", 2,
$true, -2)
$txtstream.WriteLine("<html>")
$txtstream.WriteLine("<head>")
$txtstream.WriteLine("<title>Products</title>")
$txtstream.WriteLine("<body>")
```

For Reports:

```
$txtstream.WriteLine("<table border=0 cellspacing=3 cellpadding=3>")
```

For Tables:

```
$txtstream.WriteLine("<table border=1 cellspacing=3 cellpadding=3>")

$txtstream.WriteLine("<%")
```

```
$txtstream.WriteLine("Response.Write('<tr>' & vbcrlf)")
for each($col in $dt.Columns)
{
    $txtstream.WriteLine("Response.Write('<th align='left' nowrap='nowrap'>" +
$col.Caption + "</th>' & vbcrlf)")
}
$txtstream.WriteLine("Response.Write('</tr>' & vbcrlf)")
```

Additional Tags:

None

```
foreach($dr in $dt.Rows)
{
    $txtstream.WriteLine("Response.Write('<tr>' & vbcrlf)")
    for each($col in $dt.Columns)
    {
        $txtstream.WriteLine("Response.Write('<td align='left' nowrap='nowrap'>"
+ $dr[$col.Caption].ToString() + "</td>' & vbcrlf)")
    }
    $txtstream.WriteLine("Response.Write('</tr>' & vbcrlf)")
}
```

Button

```
foreach($dr in $dt.Rows)
{
    $txtstream.WriteLine("Response.Write('<tr>' & vbcrlf)")
    for each($col in $dt.Columns)
    {
        $txtstream.WriteLine("Response.Write('<td align='left'
nowrap='true'><button style='width:100%;' value ='" + $dr[$col.Caption].ToString()
+ "'>" + $dr[$col.Caption].ToString() + "</button></td>' & vbcrlf)")
    }
    $txtstream.WriteLine("Response.Write('</tr>' & vbcrlf)")
}
```

Combobox

```
foreach($dr in $dt.Rows)
{
    $txtstream.WriteLine("Response.Write('<tr>' & vbcrlf)")
    for each($col in $dt.Columns)
    {
        $txtstream.WriteLine("Response.Write('<td align='left'
nowrap='true'><select><option value = '" + $dr[$col.Caption].ToString() + "'>" +
$dr[$col.Caption].ToString() + "</option></select></td>' & vbcrlf)")
```

```
      }
      $txtstream.WriteLine("Response.Write('</tr>' & vbcrlf)")
  }
```

Div

```
  foreach($dr in  $dt.Rows)
  {
      $txtstream.WriteLine("Response.Write('<tr>' & vbcrlf)")
      for each($col in  $dt.Columns)
      {
          $txtstream.WriteLine("Response.Write('<td  align='left'
nowrap='true'><div>" + $dr[$col.Caption].ToString() + "</div></td>' & vbcrlf)")
      }
      $txtstream.WriteLine("Response.Write('</tr>' & vbcrlf)")
  }
```

Link

```
  foreach($dr in  $dt.Rows)
  {
      $txtstream.WriteLine("Response.Write('<tr>' & vbcrlf)")
      for each($col in  $dt.Columns)
      {
          $txtstream.WriteLine("Response.Write('<td  align='left' nowrap='true'><a
href='" + $dr[$col.Caption].ToString() + "'>" + $dr[$col.Caption].ToString() +
"</a></td>' & vbcrlf)")
      }
      $txtstream.WriteLine("Response.Write('</tr>' & vbcrlf)")
  }
```

Listbox

```
  foreach($dr in  $dt.Rows)
  {
      $txtstream.WriteLine("Response.Write('<tr>' & vbcrlf)")
      for each($col in  $dt.Columns)
      {
          $txtstream.WriteLine("Response.Write('<td  align='left'
nowrap='true'><select multiple><option value = '" + $dr[$col.Caption].ToString() +
"'>" + $dr[$col.Caption].ToString() + "</option></select></td>' & vbcrlf)")
      }
      $txtstream.WriteLine("Response.Write('</tr>' & vbcrlf)")
  }
```

Span

```
foreach($dr in  $dt.Rows)
{
    $txtstream.WriteLine("Response.Write('<tr>' & vbcrlf)")
    for each($col in  $dt.Columns)
    {
       $txtstream.WriteLine("Response.Write('<td align='left'
nowrap='true'><span>" + $dr[$col.Caption].ToString() + "</span></td>' & vbcrlf)")
    }
    $txtstream.WriteLine("Response.Write('</tr>' & vbcrlf)")
}
```

Textarea

```
foreach($dr in  $dt.Rows)
{
    $txtstream.WriteLine("Response.Write('<tr>' & vbcrlf)")
    for each($col in  $dt.Columns)
    {
       $txtstream.WriteLine("Response.Write('<td align='left'
nowrap='true'><textarea>" + $dr[$col.Caption].ToString() + "</textarea></td>' &
vbcrlf)")
    }
    $txtstream.WriteLine("Response.Write('</tr>' & vbcrlf)")
}
```

Textbox

```
foreach($dr in  $dt.Rows)
{
    $txtstream.WriteLine("Response.Write('<tr>' & vbcrlf)")
    for each($col in  $dt.Columns)
    {
       $txtstream.WriteLine("Response.Write('<td  align='left'
nowrap='true'><input type=text value='" + $dr[$col.Caption].ToString() +
"'></input></td>' & vbcrlf)")
    }
    $txtstream.WriteLine("Response.Write('</tr>' & vbcrlf)")
}
```

End Code

```
$txtstream.WriteLine("%>")
$txtstream.WriteLine("</table>")
$txtstream.WriteLine("</body>")
$txtstream.WriteLine("</html>")
$txtstream.Close()
```

VERTICAL

```
$ws = new-object -com WScript.Shell
$fso = new-object -com Scripting.FileSystemObject
$txtstream = $fso.OpenTextFile($ws.CurrentDirectory + "\\Products.asp", 2,
$true, -2)
$txtstream.WriteLine("<html>")
$txtstream.WriteLine("<head>")
$txtstream.WriteLine("<title>Products</title>")
$txtstream.WriteLine("<body>")
$txtstream.WriteLine("<center>")
$txtstream.WriteLine("</br>")
$txtstream.WriteLine("</br>")
```

For Reports:

```
$txtstream.WriteLine("<table border=0 cellspacing=3 cellpadding=3>")
```

For Tables:

```
$txtstream.WriteLine("<table border=1 cellspacing=3 cellpadding=3>")

$txtstream.WriteLine("<%")
for each($col in  $dt.Columns)
{
    $txtstream.WriteLine("Response.Write('<tr><th align='left'
nowrap='nowrap'>" + $col.Caption + "</th>' & vbcrlf)")
```

None

```
foreach($dr in  $dt.Rows)
{
    $txtstream.WriteLine("Response.Write('<td  align='left' nowrap='nowrap'>"
+ $dr[$col.Caption].ToString() + "</td>' & vbcrlf)")
}
```

Additional Tags:

None

```
foreach($dr in $dt.Rows)
{
    $txtstream.WriteLine("Response.Write('<td align='left' nowrap='nowrap'>"
+ $dr[$col.Caption].ToString() + "</td>' & vbcrlf)")
}
```

Button

```
foreach($dr in $dt.Rows)
{
    $txtstream.WriteLine("Response.Write('<td align='left'
nowrap='true'><button style='width:100%;' value ='" + $dr[$col.Caption].ToString()
+ "'>" + $dr[$col.Caption].ToString() + "</button></td>' & vbcrlf)")
}
```

Combobox

```
foreach($dr in $dt.Rows)
{
    $txtstream.WriteLine("Response.Write('<td align='left'
nowrap='true'><select><option value = '" + $dr[$col.Caption].ToString() + "'>" +
$dr[$col.Caption].ToString() + "</option></select></td>' & vbcrlf)")
}
```

Div

```
foreach($dr in $dt.Rows)
{
    $txtstream.WriteLine("Response.Write('<td align='left'
nowrap='true'><div>" + $dr[$col.Caption].ToString() + "</div></td>' & vbcrlf)")
}
```

Link

```
foreach($dr in $dt.Rows)
{
    $txtstream.WriteLine("Response.Write('<td align='left' nowrap='true'><a
href='" + $dr[$col.Caption].ToString() + "'>" + $dr[$col.Caption].ToString() +
"</a></td>' & vbcrlf)")
}
```

Listbox

```
foreach($dr in $dt.Rows)
{
```

```
    $txtstream.WriteLine("Response.Write('<td  align='left'
nowrap='true'><select multiple><option value = '" + $dr[$col.Caption].ToString() +
'">" + $dr[$col.Caption].ToString() + "</option></select></td>' & vbcrlf)")
    }
```

Span

```
    foreach($dr in  $dt.Rows)
    {
        $txtstream.WriteLine("Response.Write('<td  align='left'
nowrap='true'><span>" + $dr[$col.Caption].ToString() + "</span></td>' & vbcrlf)")
    }
```

Textarea

```
    foreach($dr in  $dt.Rows)
    {
        $txtstream.WriteLine("Response.Write('<td  align='left'
nowrap='true'><textarea>" + $dr[$col.Caption].ToString() + "</textarea></td>' &
vbcrlf)")
    }
```

Textbox

```
    foreach($dr in  $dt.Rows)
    {
        $txtstream.WriteLine("Response.Write('<td  align='left'
nowrap='true'><input type=text value='" + $dr[$col.Caption].ToString() +
'"></input></td>' & vbcrlf)")
    }
```

End Code

```
    $txtstream.WriteLine("Response.Write('</tr>' & vbcrlf)")
  }
  $txtstream.WriteLine("%>")
  $txtstream.WriteLine("</table>")
  $txtstream.WriteLine("</body>")
  $txtstream.WriteLine("</html>")
  $txtstream.Close()
```

HTA EXAMPLES

Back to the future!

B elow, are examples of using SQL CLIENT, the Datatable and HTA. And just in case you are wondering, I use none as meaning no additional tags between the <td></td>.

HORIZONTAL

```
$ws = new-object -com WScript.Shell
$fso = new-object -com Scripting.FileSystemObject
$txtstream = $fso.OpenTextFile($ws.CurrentDirectory + "\\Products.hta", 2,
$true, -2)
$txtstream.WriteLine("<html>")
$txtstream.WriteLine("<head>")
$txtstream.WriteLine("<HTA:APPLICATION ")
$txtstream.WriteLine("ID = 'Products' ")
$txtstream.WriteLine("APPLICATIONNAME = 'Products' ")
$txtstream.WriteLine("SCROLL = 'yes' ")
$txtstream.WriteLine("SINGLEINSTANCE = 'yes' ")
$txtstream.WriteLine("WINDOWSTATE = 'maximize' >")
$txtstream.WriteLine("<title>Products</title>")
$txtstream.WriteLine("<body>")
```

For Reports:

```
$txtstream.WriteLine("<table border=0 cellspacing=3 cellpadding=3>")
```

For Tables:

```
$txtstream.WriteLine("<table border=1 cellspacing=3 cellpadding=3>")

$txtstream.WriteLine("<tr>")
for each($col in  $dt.Columns)
{
    $txtstream.WriteLine("<th align='left' nowrap='nowrap'>" +    $col.Caption +
"</th>")
}
$txtstream.WriteLine("</tr>")
```

Additional Tags:

None

```
foreach($dr in  $dt.Rows)
{
    $txtstream.WriteLine("<tr>")
    for each($col in  $dt.Columns)
    {
        $txtstream.WriteLine("<td  align='left' nowrap='nowrap'>" +
$dr[$col.Caption].ToString() + "</td>")
    }
    $txtstream.WriteLine("</tr>")
}
```

Button

```
foreach($dr in  $dt.Rows)
{
    $txtstream.WriteLine("<tr>")
    for each($col in  $dt.Columns)
    {
        $txtstream.WriteLine("<td  align='left' nowrap='true'><button
style='width:100%;' value ='" + $dr[$col.Caption].ToString() + "'>" +
$dr[$col.Caption].ToString() + "</button></td>")
    }
    $txtstream.WriteLine("</tr>")
}
```

Combobox

```
foreach($dr in  $dt.Rows)
{
```

```
$txtstream.WriteLine("<tr>")
for each($col in $dt.Columns)
{
    $txtstream.WriteLine("<td align='left' nowrap='true'><select><option value
= '" + $dr[$col.Caption].ToString() + "'>" + $dr[$col.Caption].ToString() +
"</option></select></td>")
}
$txtstream.WriteLine("</tr>")
}
```

Div

```
foreach($dr in $dt.Rows)
{
    $txtstream.WriteLine("<tr>")
    for each($col in $dt.Columns)
    {
        $txtstream.WriteLine("<td align='left' nowrap='true'><div>" +
$dr[$col.Caption].ToString() + "</div></td>")
    }
    $txtstream.WriteLine("</tr>")
}
```

Link

```
foreach($dr in $dt.Rows)
{
    $txtstream.WriteLine("<tr>")
    for each($col in $dt.Columns)
    {
        $txtstream.WriteLine("<td align='left' nowrap='true'><a href='" +
$dr[$col.Caption].ToString() + "'>" + $dr[$col.Caption].ToString() + "</a></td>")
    }
    $txtstream.WriteLine("</tr>")
}
```

Listbox

```
foreach($dr in $dt.Rows)
{
    $txtstream.WriteLine("<tr>")
    for each($col in $dt.Columns)
    {
        $txtstream.WriteLine("<td align='left' nowrap='true'><select
multiple><option value = '" + $dr[$col.Caption].ToString() + "'>" +
$dr[$col.Caption].ToString() + "</option></select></td>")
    }
```

```
      $txtstream.WriteLine("</tr>")
   }
```

Span

```
   foreach($dr in  $dt.Rows)
   {
      $txtstream.WriteLine("<tr>")
      for each($col in  $dt.Columns)
      {
         $txtstream.WriteLine("<td align='left' nowrap='true'><span>" +
$dr[$col.Caption].ToString() + "</span></td>")
      }
      $txtstream.WriteLine("</tr>")
   }
```

Textarea

```
   foreach($dr in  $dt.Rows)
   {
      $txtstream.WriteLine("<tr>")
      for each($col in  $dt.Columns)
      {
         $txtstream.WriteLine("<td align='left' nowrap='true'><textarea>" +
$dr[$col.Caption].ToString() + "</textarea></td>")
      }
      $txtstream.WriteLine("</tr>")
   }
```

Textbox

```
   foreach($dr in  $dt.Rows)
   {
      $txtstream.WriteLine("<tr>")
      for each($col in  $dt.Columns)
      {
         $txtstream.WriteLine("<td align='left' nowrap='true'><input type=text
value='" + $dr[$col.Caption].ToString() + "'></input></td>")
      }
      $txtstream.WriteLine("</tr>")
   }
```

End Code

```
   $txtstream.WriteLine("</table>")
   $txtstream.WriteLine("</body>")
   $txtstream.WriteLine("</html>")
```

```
$txtstream.Close()
```

VERTICAL

```
$ws = new-object -com WScript.Shell
$fso = new-object -com Scripting.FileSystemObject
$txtstream = $fso.OpenTextFile($ws.CurrentDirectory + "\\Products.hta", 2,
$true, -2)
$txtstream.WriteLine("<html>")
$txtstream.WriteLine("<head>")
$txtstream.WriteLine("<title>Products</title>")
$txtstream.WriteLine("<body>")
$txtstream.WriteLine("<center>")
$txtstream.WriteLine("</br>")
$txtstream.WriteLine("</br>")
```

For Reports:

```
$txtstream.WriteLine("<table border=0 cellspacing=3 cellpadding=3>")
```

For Tables:

```
$txtstream.WriteLine("<table border=1 cellspacing=3 cellpadding=3>")
```

```
for each($col in $dt.Columns)
{
    $txtstream.WriteLine("<tr><th align='left' nowrap='nowrap'>" + $col.Caption
+ "</th>")
```

Additional Tags:

None

```
foreach($dr in $dt.Rows)
{
    $txtstream.WriteLine("<td align='left' nowrap='nowrap'>" +
$dr[$col.Caption].ToString() + "</td>")
}
```

Button

```
foreach($dr in $dt.Rows)
{
```

```
    $txtstream.WriteLine("<td  align='left' nowrap='true'><button
style='width:100%;' value ='" + $dr[$col.Caption].ToString() + "'>" +
$dr[$col.Caption].ToString() + "</button></td>“)
    }
```

Combobox

```
    foreach($dr in  $dt.Rows)
    {
        $txtstream.WriteLine("<td  align='left' nowrap='true'><select><option value
= '" + $dr[$col.Caption].ToString() + "'>" + $dr[$col.Caption].ToString() +
"</option></select></td>“)
    }
```

Div

```
    foreach($dr in  $dt.Rows)
    {
        $txtstream.WriteLine("<td  align='left' nowrap='true'><div>" +
$dr[$col.Caption].ToString() + "</div></td>“)
    }
```

Link

```
    foreach($dr in  $dt.Rows)
    {
        $txtstream.WriteLine("<td  align='left' nowrap='true'><a href='" +
$dr[$col.Caption].ToString() + "'>" + $dr[$col.Caption].ToString() + "</a></td>“)
    }
```

Listbox

```
    foreach($dr in  $dt.Rows)
    {
        $txtstream.WriteLine("<td  align='left' nowrap='true'><select
multiple><option value = '" + $dr[$col.Caption].ToString() + "'>" +
$dr[$col.Caption].ToString() + "</option></select></td>“)
    }
```
Span

```
    foreach($dr in  $dt.Rows)
    {
        $txtstream.WriteLine("<td  align='left' nowrap='true'><span>" +
$dr[$col.Caption].ToString() + "</span></td>“)
    }
```

```
foreach($dr in  $dt.Rows)
{
    $txtstream.WriteLine("<td  align='left' nowrap='true'><textarea>" +
$dr[$col.Caption].ToString() + "</textarea></td>")
}
```

```
foreach($dr in  $dt.Rows)
{
    $txtstream.WriteLine("<td  align='left' nowrap='true'><input type=text
value='" + $dr[$col.Caption].ToString() + "'></input></td>")
}
```

```
    $txtstream.WriteLine("</tr>")
}
$txtstream.WriteLine("</table>")
$txtstream.WriteLine("</body>")
$txtstream.WriteLine("</html>")
$txtstream.Close()
```

HTML EXAMPLES

Let there be HTML!

Below, are examples of using SQL CLIENT, the Datatable and HTML. And just in case you are wondering, I use none as meaning no additional tags between the <td></td>.

HORIZONTAL

```
$ws = new-object -com WScript.Shell
$fso = new-object -com Scripting.FileSystemObject
$txtstream = $fso.OpenTextFile($ws.CurrentDirectory + "\\Products.html", 2,
$true, -2)
  $txtstream.WriteLine("<html>")
  $txtstream.WriteLine("<head>")
  $txtstream.WriteLine("<title>Products</title>")
  $txtstream.WriteLine("<body>")
```

For Reports:

```
  $txtstream.WriteLine("<table border=0 cellspacing=3 cellpadding=3>")
```

For Tables:

```
  $txtstream.WriteLine("<table border=1 cellspacing=3 cellpadding=3>")
```

```
$txtstream.WriteLine("<%")
$txtstream.WriteLine("<tr>")
for each($col in $dt.Columns)
{
    $txtstream.WriteLine("<th align='left' nowrap='nowrap'>" +    $col.Caption +
"</th>")
}
$txtstream.WriteLine("</tr>")
```

Additional Tags:

None

```
foreach($dr in $dt.Rows)
{
    $txtstream.WriteLine("<tr>")
    for each($col in $dt.Columns)
    {
        $txtstream.WriteLine("<td align='left' nowrap='nowrap'>" +
$dr[$col.Caption].ToString() + "</td>")
    }
    $txtstream.WriteLine("</tr>")
}
```

Button

```
foreach($dr in $dt.Rows)
{
    $txtstream.WriteLine("<tr>")
    for each($col in $dt.Columns)
    {
        $txtstream.WriteLine("<td align='left' nowrap='true'><button
style='width:100%;' value ='" + $dr[$col.Caption].ToString() + "'>" +
$dr[$col.Caption].ToString() + "</button></td>")
    }
    $txtstream.WriteLine("</tr>")
}
```

Combobox

```
foreach($dr in $dt.Rows)
{
    $txtstream.WriteLine("<tr>")
    for each($col in $dt.Columns)
    {
```

```
        $txtstream.WriteLine("<td align='left' nowrap='true'><select><option value
= '" + $dr[$col.Caption].ToString() + "'>" + $dr[$col.Caption].ToString() +
"</option></select></td>")
      }
    $txtstream.WriteLine("</tr>")
  }
```

Div

```
  foreach($dr in  $dt.Rows)
  {
    $txtstream.WriteLine("<tr>")
    for each($col in  $dt.Columns)
    {
      $txtstream.WriteLine("<td align='left' nowrap='true'><div>" +
$dr[$col.Caption].ToString() + "</div></td>")
    }
    $txtstream.WriteLine("</tr>")
  }
```

Link

```
  foreach($dr in  $dt.Rows)
  {
    $txtstream.WriteLine("<tr>")
    for each($col in  $dt.Columns)
    {
      $txtstream.WriteLine("<td align='left' nowrap='true'><a href='" +
$dr[$col.Caption].ToString() + "'>" + $dr[$col.Caption].ToString() + "</a></td>")
    }
    $txtstream.WriteLine("</tr>")
  }
```

Listbox

```
  foreach($dr in  $dt.Rows)
  {
    $txtstream.WriteLine("<tr>")
    for each($col in  $dt.Columns)
    {
      $txtstream.WriteLine("<td align='left' nowrap='true'><select
multiple><option value = '" + $dr[$col.Caption].ToString() + "'>" +
$dr[$col.Caption].ToString() + "</option></select></td>")
    }
    $txtstream.WriteLine("</tr>")
  }
```

```
foreach($dr in $dt.Rows)
{
    $txtstream.WriteLine("<tr>")
    for each($col in $dt.Columns)
    {
        $txtstream.WriteLine("<td align='left' nowrap='true'><span>" +
$dr[$col.Caption].ToString() + "</span></td>")
    }
    $txtstream.WriteLine("</tr>")
}
```

```
foreach($dr in $dt.Rows)
{
    $txtstream.WriteLine("<tr>")
    for each($col in $dt.Columns)
    {
        $txtstream.WriteLine("<td align='left' nowrap='true'><textarea>" +
$dr[$col.Caption].ToString() + "</textarea></td>")
    }
    $txtstream.WriteLine("</tr>")
}
```

```
foreach($dr in $dt.Rows)
{
    $txtstream.WriteLine("<tr>")
    for each($col in $dt.Columns)
    {
        $txtstream.WriteLine("<td align='left' nowrap='true'><input type=text
value='" + $dr[$col.Caption].ToString() + "'></input></td>")
    }
    $txtstream.WriteLine("</tr>")
}
```

```
$txtstream.WriteLine("%>")
$txtstream.WriteLine("</table>")
$txtstream.WriteLine("</body>")
$txtstream.WriteLine("</html>")
$txtstream.Close()
```

VERTICAL

```
$ws = new-object -com WScript.Shell
$fso = new-object -com Scripting.FileSystemObject
$txtstream = $fso.OpenTextFile($ws.CurrentDirectory + "\\Products.html", 2,
$true, -2)
$txtstream.WriteLine("<html>")
$txtstream.WriteLine("<head>")
$txtstream.WriteLine("<title>Products</title>")
$txtstream.WriteLine("<body>")
$txtstream.WriteLine("<center>")
$txtstream.WriteLine("</br>")
$txtstream.WriteLine("</br>")
```

For Reports:

```
$txtstream.WriteLine("<table border=0 cellspacing=3 cellpadding=3>")
```

For Tables:

```
$txtstream.WriteLine("<table border=1 cellspacing=3 cellpadding=3>")

for each($col in $dt.Columns)
{
    $txtstream.WriteLine("<tr><th align='left' nowrap='nowrap'>" + $col.Caption
+ "</th>")
```

Additional Tags:

None

```
    foreach($dr in $dt.Rows)
    {
        $txtstream.WriteLine("<td  align='left' nowrap='nowrap'>" +
$dr[$col.Caption].ToString() + "</td>")
    }
```

Button

```
    foreach($dr in $dt.Rows)
    {
```

```
        $txtstream.WriteLine("<td align='left' nowrap='true'><button
style='width:100%;' value ='" + $dr[$col.Caption].ToString() + "'>" +
$dr[$col.Caption].ToString() + "</button></td>")
    }
```

Combobox

```
    foreach($dr in $dt.Rows)
    {
        $txtstream.WriteLine("<td align='left' nowrap='true'><select><option value
= '" + $dr[$col.Caption].ToString() + "'>" + $dr[$col.Caption].ToString() +
"</option></select></td>")
    }
```

Div

```
    foreach($dr in $dt.Rows)
    {
        $txtstream.WriteLine("<td align='left' nowrap='true'><div>" +
$dr[$col.Caption].ToString() + "</div></td>")
    }
```

Link

```
    foreach($dr in $dt.Rows)
    {
        $txtstream.WriteLine("<td align='left' nowrap='true'><a href='" +
$dr[$col.Caption].ToString() + "'>" + $dr[$col.Caption].ToString() + "</a></td>")
    }
```

Listbox

```
    foreach($dr in $dt.Rows)
    {
        $txtstream.WriteLine("<td align='left' nowrap='true'><select
multiple><option value = '" + $dr[$col.Caption].ToString() + "'>" +
$dr[$col.Caption].ToString() + "</option></select></td>")
    }
```
Span

```
    foreach($dr in $dt.Rows)
    {
        $txtstream.WriteLine("<td align='left' nowrap='true'><span>" +
$dr[$col.Caption].ToString() + "</span></td>")
    }
```

```
    foreach($dr in  $dt.Rows)
    {
        $txtstream.WriteLine("<td  align='left' nowrap='true'><textarea>" +
$dr[$col.Caption].ToString() + "</textarea></td>")
    }
```

```
    foreach($dr in  $dt.Rows)
    {
        $txtstream.WriteLine("<td  align='left' nowrap='true'><input type=text
value='" + $dr[$col.Caption].ToString() + "'></input></td>")
    }
```

```
    $txtstream.WriteLine("</tr>")
  }
  $txtstream.WriteLine("</table>")
  $txtstream.WriteLine("</body>")
  $txtstream.WriteLine("</html>")
  $txtstream.Close()
```

DELIMITED TEXT FILES

B ELOW ARE THE POPULAR EXAMPLES OF DIFFERENT DELIMITED TEXT FILES.

COLON DELIMITED HORIZONTAL VIEW

```
$tempstr = ""

$ws = new-object -com WScript.Shell
$fso = new-object -com Scripting.FileSystemObject
$txtstream = $fso.OpenTextFile($ws.CurrentDirectory + "\Products.txt", 2, $true,
-2)
for each($col in  $dt.Columns)
{
   if ($tempstr != "")
   {
      $tempstr = $tempstr + ":"
   }
   $tempstr = $tempstr + $col.Caption;
}
$txtstream.WriteLine($tempstr)
$tempstr = ""

foreach($dr in  $dt.rows)
{
   for each($col in  $dt.Columns)
   {
      if ($tempstr != "")
      {
```

```
            $tempstr = $tempstr + ":"
        }
            $tempstr = $tempstr + "" + $dr[$col.Caption].ToString() + ""
        }
        $txtstream.WriteLine($tempstr)
        $tempstr = ""

}
$txtstream.Close()
```

COLON DELIMITED VERTICAL VIEW

```
System.String^ $tempstr = ""

    $tempstr = ""

    $ws = new-object -com WScript.Shell
    $fso = new-object -com Scripting.FileSystemObject
    $txtstream = $fso.OpenTextFile($ws.CurrentDirectory + "\Products.txt", 2, $true,
-2)
for each($col in $dt.Columns)
{
    $tempstr = $col.Caption;
    foreach($dr in $dt.rows)
    {
        if ($tempstr != "")
        {
            $tempstr = $tempstr + ":"
        }
            $tempstr = $tempstr + "" + $dr[$col.Caption].ToString() + ""
        }
    }
    $txtstream.WriteLine($tempstr)
    $tempstr = ""

}
$txtstream.Close()
```

COMMA DELIMITED HORIZONTAL VIEW

```
    $tempstr = ""

    $ws = new-object -com WScript.Shell
    $fso = new-object -com Scripting.FileSystemObject
```

```
$txtstream = $fso.OpenTextFile($ws.CurrentDirectory + "\Products.csv", 2, $true, -
2)
for each($col in $dt.Columns)
{
   if ($tempstr != "")
   {
      $tempstr = $tempstr + ","
   }
   $tempstr = $tempstr + $col.Caption;
}
$txtstream.WriteLine($tempstr)
$tempstr = ""

foreach($dr in $dt.rows)
{
   for each($col in $dt.Columns)
   {
      if ($tempstr != "")
      {
         $tempstr = $tempstr + ","
      }
         $tempstr = $tempstr + "" + $dr[$col.Caption].ToString() + ""
      }
      $txtstream.WriteLine($tempstr)
      $tempstr = ""

}
$txtstream.Close()
```

COMMA DELIMITED VERTICAL VIEW

```
   $tempstr = ""

   $ws = new-object -com WScript.Shell
   $fso = new-object -com Scripting.FileSystemObject
   $txtstream = $fso.OpenTextFile($ws.CurrentDirectory + "\Products.csv", 2, $true,
   -2)
for each($col in $dt.Columns)
{
   $tempstr = $col.Caption;
   foreach($dr in $dt.rows)
   {
      if ($tempstr != "")
      {
         $tempstr = $tempstr + ","
      }
```

```
      $tempstr = $tempstr + """ + $dr[$col.Caption].ToString() + """
   }
   }
   $txtstream.WriteLine($tempstr)
   $tempstr = """

}
$txtstream.Close()
```

EXCLAMATION DELIMITED HORIZONTAL VIEW

```
   $tempstr = """

   $ws = new-object -com WScript.Shell
   $fso = new-object -com Scripting.FileSystemObject
   $txtstream = $fso.OpenTextFile($ws.CurrentDirectory + "\Products.txt", 2, $true,
-2)
for each($col in $dt.Columns)
{
   if ($tempstr != """)
   {
      $tempstr = $tempstr + "!"
   }
   $tempstr = $tempstr + $col.Caption;
}
$txtstream.WriteLine($tempstr)
$tempstr = """

foreach($dr in $dt.rows)
{
   for each($col in $dt.Columns)
   {
      if ($tempstr != """)
      {
         $tempstr = $tempstr + "!"
      }
      $tempstr = $tempstr + """ + $dr[$col.Caption].ToString() + """
      }
      $txtstream.WriteLine($tempstr)
      $tempstr = """

}
$txtstream.Close()
```

EXCLAMATION DELIMITED VERTICAL VIEW

```
$tempstr = ""

$ws = new-object -com WScript.Shell
$fso = new-object -com Scripting.FileSystemObject
$txtstream = $fso.OpenTextFile($ws.CurrentDirectory + "\Products.txt", 2, $true,
-2)
for each($col in $dt.Columns)
{
   $tempstr = $col.Caption;
   foreach($dr in $dt.rows)
   {
      if ($tempstr != "")
      {
         $tempstr = $tempstr + "!"
      }
         $tempstr = $tempstr + "" + $dr[$col.Caption].ToString() + ""
   }
   $txtstream.WriteLine($tempstr)
   $tempstr = ""

}
$txtstream.Close()
```

SEMI-COLON DELIMITED HORIZONTAL VIEW

```
$tempstr = ""

$ws = new-object -com WScript.Shell
$fso = new-object -com Scripting.FileSystemObject
$txtstream = $fso.OpenTextFile($ws.CurrentDirectory + "\Products.txt", 2, $true,
-2)
for each($col in $dt.Columns)
{
   if ($tempstr != "")
   {
      $tempstr = $tempstr + ";"
   }
   $tempstr = $tempstr + $col.Caption;
}
$txtstream.WriteLine($tempstr)
$tempstr = ""
```

```
foreach($dr in  $dt.rows)
{
   for each($col in  $dt.Columns)
   {
     if ($tempstr != "")
     {
       $tempstr = $tempstr + ";"
     }
       $tempstr = $tempstr + "" + $dr[$col.Caption].ToString() + ""
     }
     $txtstream.WriteLine($tempstr)
     $tempstr = ""

}
$txtstream.Close()
```

SEMI-COLON DELIMITED VERTICAL VIEW

```
   $tempstr = ""


  $ws = new-object -com WScript.Shell
  $fso = new-object -com Scripting.FileSystemObject
  $txtstream = $fso.OpenTextFile($ws.CurrentDirectory + "\Products.txt", 2, $true,
-2)
for each($col in  $dt.Columns)
{
   $tempstr = $col.Caption;
   foreach($dr in  $dt.rows)
   {
     if ($tempstr != "")
     {
       $tempstr = $tempstr + ";"
     }
       $tempstr = $tempstr + "" + $dr[$col.Caption].ToString() + ""
     }
   }
   $txtstream.WriteLine($tempstr)
   $tempstr = ""

}
$txtstream.Close()
```

TAB DELIMITED HORIZONTAL VIEW

```
    $tempstr = ""

  $ws = new-object -com WScript.Shell
  $fso = new-object -com Scripting.FileSystemObject
  $txtstream = $fso.OpenTextFile($ws.CurrentDirectory + "\Products.txt", 2, $true,
-2)
for each($col in  $dt.Columns)
{
  if ($tempstr != "")
  {
     $tempstr = $tempstr + "\t"
  }
  $tempstr = $tempstr + $col.Caption;
}
$txtstream.WriteLine($tempstr)
$tempstr = ""

foreach($dr in  $dt.rows)
{
  for each($col in  $dt.Columns)
  {
    if ($tempstr != "")
    {
       $tempstr = $tempstr + "\t"
    }
       $tempstr = $tempstr + "" + $dr[$col.Caption].ToString() + ""
    }
    $txtstream.WriteLine($tempstr)
    $tempstr = ""

}
$txtstream.Close()
```

TAB DELIMITED VERTICAL VIEW

```
    $tempstr = ""

  $ws = new-object -com WScript.Shell
  $fso = new-object -com Scripting.FileSystemObject
  $txtstream = $fso.OpenTextFile($ws.CurrentDirectory + "\Products.txt", 2, $true,
-2)
for each($col in  $dt.Columns)
{
  $tempstr = $col.Caption;
  foreach($dr in  $dt.rows)
  {
    if ($tempstr != "")
```

```
      {
        $tempstr = $tempstr + "\t"
      }
        $tempstr = $tempstr + "" + $dr[$col.Caption].ToString() + ""
      }
    }
    $txtstream.WriteLine($tempstr)
    $tempstr = ""

}
$txtstream.Close()
```

TILDE DELIMITED HORIZONTAL VIEW

```
$tempstr = ""

$ws = new-object -com WScript.Shell
$fso = new-object -com Scripting.FileSystemObject
$txtstream = $fso.OpenTextFile($ws.CurrentDirectory + "\Products.txt", 2, $true, -2)
for each($col in  $dt.Columns)
{
  if ($tempstr != "")
  {
    $tempstr = $tempstr + "~"
  }
  $tempstr = $tempstr + $col.Caption
}
$txtstream.WriteLine($tempstr)
$tempstr = ""

foreach($dr in  $dt.rows)
{
  for each($col in  $dt.Columns)
  {
    if ($tempstr != "")
    {
      $tempstr = $tempstr + "~"
    }
      $tempstr = $tempstr + "" + $dr[$col.Caption].ToString() + ""
    }
    $txtstream.WriteLine($tempstr)
    $tempstr = ""

}
$txtstream.Close()
```

TILDE DELIMITED VERTICAL VIEW

```
$tempstr = ""

$ws = new-object -com WScript.Shell
$fso = new-object -com Scripting.FileSystemObject
$txtstream = $fso.OpenTextFile($ws.CurrentDirectory + "\Products.txt", 2, $true, -
2)
for each($col in  $dt.Columns)
{
   $tempstr = $col.Caption;
   foreach($dr in  $dt.rows)
   {
     if ($tempstr != "")
     {
        $tempstr = $tempstr ı " .";
     }
        $tempstr = $tempstr + "" + $dr[$col.Caption].ToString() + ""
     }
   }
   $txtstream.WriteLine($tempstr)
   $tempstr = ""

}
$txtstream.Close()
```

WORKING EXCEL

The Tale of three ways you can do it

BELOW ARE THREE EXAMPLES ON HOW TO WORK WITH EXCEL. The first will need a reference to Microsoft Excel.

HORIZONTAL AUTOMATION

```
$oExcel = new-object Excel.Application()
$oExcel.Visible = $true
$wb = $oExcel.Workbooks.Add()
$ws = wb.Worksheets[1]
$ws.Name = "Products"

$x = 1;
$y = 2;


for each($col in  $dt.Columns)
{
   $ws.Cells[1, $x] = $col.Caption;
```

```
      $x=$x+1;
    }
    $x = 1;
    foreach($dr in  $dt.rows)
    {
        for each($col in  $dt.Columns)
        {
            $ws.Cells[$y, $x] = $dr[$col.Caption].ToString()
            $x= $x + 1
        }
        $x = 1
        $y = $y + 1
    }
    $ws.Columns.HorizontalAlignment = -4131
    $ws.Columns.AutoFit()
```

VERTICAL AUTOMATION

```
    $oExcel = new-object Excel.Application()
    $oExcel.Visible = $true
    $wb = $oExcel.Workbooks.Add()
    $ws = wb.Worksheets[1]
    $ws.Name = "Products"

    $x = 1;
    $y = 2;


    for each($col in  $dt.Columns)
    {
        $ws.Cells[$x, 1] = $col.Caption;
        $x=$x+1;
    }
    $x = 1;
    foreach($dr in  $dt.rows)
    {
        for each($col in  $dt.Columns)
        {
            $ws.Cells[$x, $y] = $dr[$col.Caption].ToString()
            $x= $x + 1
        }
        $x = 1
        $y = $y + 1
    }
    $ws.Columns.HorizontalAlignment = -4131
    $ws.Columns.AutoFit()
```

SPREADSHEET

```
$ws = new-object -com WScript.Shell
$fso = new-object -com Scripting.FileSystemObject
$txtstream = $fso.OpenTextFile($ws.CurrentDirectory + "\Products.xml", 2, $true, -
2)
$txtstream.WriteLine("<?xml version='1.0'?>")
$txtstream.WriteLine("<?mso-application progid='Excel.Sheet'?>")
$txtstream.WriteLine("<Workbook xmlns='urn:schemas-microsoft-
com:office:spreadsheet' xmlns:o='urn:schemas-microsoft-com:office:office'
xmlns:x='urn:schemas-microsoft-com:office:excel' xmlns:ss='urn:schemas-
microsoft-com:office:spreadsheet' xmlns:html='http://www.w3.org/TR/REC-
html40'>")
$txtstream.WriteLine("  <ExcelWorkbook xmlns='urn:schemas-microsoft-
com:office:excel'>")
$txtstream.WriteLine("      <WindowHeight>11835</WindowHeight>")
$txtstream.WriteLine("      <WindowWidth>18960</WindowWidth>")
$txtstream.WriteLine("      <WindowTopX>120</WindowTopX>")
$txtstream.WriteLine("      <WindowTopY>135</WindowTopY>")
$txtstream.WriteLine("      <Protec$tstructure>False</Protec$tstructure>")
$txtstream.WriteLine("      <ProtectWindows>False</ProtectWindows>")
$txtstream.WriteLine("  </ExcelWorkbook>")
$txtstream.WriteLine("  <Styles>")
$txtstream.WriteLine("          <Style ss:ID='s62'>")
$txtstream.WriteLine("              <Borders/>")
$txtstream.WriteLine("              <Font ss:FontName='Calibri'
x:Family='Swiss' ss:Size='11' ss:Color='#000000' ss:Bold='1'/>")
$txtstream.WriteLine("          </Style>")
$txtstream.WriteLine("          <Style ss:ID='s63'>")
$txtstream.WriteLine("              <Alignment ss:Horizontal='Left'
ss:VERTICAL='Bottom' ss:Indent='2'/>")
$txtstream.WriteLine("              <Font ss:FontName='Verdana'
x:Family='Swiss' ss:Size='7.7' ss:Color='#000000'/>")
$txtstream.WriteLine("          </Style>")
$txtstream.WriteLine("  </Styles>")
$txtstream.WriteLine("  <Worksheet ss:Name='Win32_NetworkAdapter'>")
$txtstream.WriteLine("    <Table x:FullColumns='1' x:FullRows='1'
ss:DefaultRowHeight='24.9375'>")
$txtstream.WriteLine("     <Column ss:AutoFitWidth='1' ss:Width='82.5'
ss:Span='5'/>")
$txtstream.WriteLine("     <Row ss:AutoFitHeight='0'>")
for each($col in $dt.Columns)
```

```
{
    $txtstream.WriteLine("        <Cell ss:StyleID='s62'><Data ss:Type='String'>" +
$col.Caption + "</Data></Cell>")
}
$txtstream.WriteLine("    </Row>")
foreach($dr in  $dt.rows)
{
    $txtstream.WriteLine("    <Row ss:AutoFitHeight='0'>")
    for each($col in  $dt.Columns)
    {
        $txtstream.WriteLine("        <Cell ss:StyleID='s63'><Data ss:Type='String'>" +
$dr[$col.Caption].ToString() + "</Data></Cell>")
    }
     $txtstream.WriteLine("    </Row>")
}
$txtstream.WriteLine("  </Table>")
$txtstream.WriteLine("  </Worksheet>")
$txtstream.WriteLine("</Workbook>")
$txtstream.Close()
```

HORIZONTAL CSV

```
$tempstr = ""

$ws = new-object -com WScript.Shell
$fso = new-object -com Scripting.FileSystemObject
$txtstream = $fso.OpenTextFile($ws.CurrentDirectory + "\Products.csv", 2, $true, -
2)
for each($col in  $dt.Columns)
{
    if ($tempstr != "")
    {
        $tempstr = $tempstr + ","
    }
    $tempstr = $tempstr + $col.Caption
}
$txtstream.WriteLine($tempstr)
$tempstr = ""

foreach($dr in  $dt.rows)
{
    for each($col in  $dt.Columns)
    {
        if ($tempstr != "")
        {
            $tempstr = $tempstr + ","
        }
```

```
        $tempstr = $tempstr + '"' + $dr[$col.Caption].ToString() + '"'
    }
    $txtstream.WriteLine($tempstr)
    $tempstr = ""
}
$txtstream.Close()

$ws.Run($ws.CurrentDirectory + "\\Products.csv")
```

VERTICAL CSV

```
$tempstr = ""

$ws = new-object -com WScript.Shell
$fso = new-object -com Scripting.FileSystemObject
$txtstream = $fso.OpenTextFile($ws.CurrentDirectory + "\Products.csv", 2, $true, -2)
+ "\Products.csv", 2, $true, -2)
for each($col in $dt.Columns)
{
    $tempstr = $col.Caption;
    foreach($dr in $dt.rows)
    {
        if ($tempstr != "")
        {
            $tempstr = $tempstr + ","
        }
            $tempstr = $tempstr + '"' + $dr[$col.Caption].ToString() + '"'
    }
    $txtstream.WriteLine($tempstr)
    $tempstr = ""

}
$txtstream.Close()
$ws.Run($ws.CurrentDirectory + "\\Products.csv")
```

XML Files

B ELOW ARE XML CODING EXAMPLES IN TEXT AND DOM NOTATION FOR ATTRIBUTE XML, ELEMENT XML, ELEMENT XML FOR XSL AND SCHEMA XML.

TEXT CREATED ATTRIBUTE XML

```
$ws = new-object -com WScript.Shell
$fso = new-object -com Scripting.FileSystemObject
$txtstream = $fso.OpenTextFile($ws.CurrentDirectory + "\\Products.xml", 2, $true,
-2)
    $txtstream.WriteLine("<?xml version='1.0' encoding='iso-8859-1'?>")
    $txtstream.WriteLine("<data>")
    foreach($dr in $dt.rows)
    {
      $txtstream.WriteLine("<products>")
      for each($col in $dt.Columns)
      {
        string $tstr ="";
        $tstr = "<property name =' + $col.Caption + "' ";
        $tstr = $tstr + " datatype = ' + col.DataType.Name + "' ";
        $tstr = $tstr + " length =' + $dr[$col.Caption].ToString().Length + "' ";
        $tstr = $tstr + " value =' + dr[$col.Caption] + "'/>";
        $txtstream.WriteLine($tstr)
      }
      $txtstream.WriteLine("</products>")
    }
    $txtstream.WriteLine("</data>")
    $txtstream.Close()
```

DOM CREATED ATTRIBUTE XML

```
$ws = new-object -com WScript.Shell
$xmldoc = new-object -com MSXML2.DomDocument();
$pi = xmldoc.CreateProcessingInstruction("xml", "version='1.0' encoding='iso-
8895-1'")
$oRoot = $xmldoc.CreateElement("data")
$xmldoc.AppendChild($pi);
foreach ($dr in  $dt.Rows)
{
   $oNode = $xmldoc.CreateNode(0, "Products")
   foreach ( $col in  $dt.Columns)
   {
      $oNode1 = $xmldoc.CreateNode(0, "Property")
      $oatt = $xmldoc.CreateAttribute("Name")
      $oatt.Value = $col.Caption
      $oNode1.Attributes.SetNamedItem($oatt)
      $oatt = $xmldoc.CreateAttribute("datatype")
      $oatt.Value = $col.DataType.Name
      $oNode1.Attributes.SetNamedItem($oatt)
      $oatt = $xmldoc.CreateAttribute("size")
      $oatt.Value = $dr[$col.Caption].ToString().Length.ToString()
      $oNode1.Attributes.SetNamedItem($oatt)
      $oatt = $xmldoc.CreateAttribute("value")
      $oatt.Value = $dr[$col.Caption].ToString()
      $oNode1.Attributes.SetNamedItem($oatt)
      $oNode.AppendChild($oNode1)
   }
   $oRoot.AppendChild($oNode)
}
$xmldoc.AppendChild($oRoot);
$xmldoc.Save($ws.CurrentDirectory + "\\Products.xml")
```

TEXT CREATED ELEMENT XML

```
$ws = new-object -com WScript.Shell
$fso = new-object -com Scripting.FileSystemObject
$txtstream = $fso.OpenTextFile($ws.CurrentDirectory + "\\Products.xml", 2, $true,
-2)
$txtstream.WriteLine("<?xml version='1.0' encoding='iso-8859-1'?>")
$txtstream.WriteLine("<data>")
foreach($dr in $dt.rows)
{
   $txtstream.WriteLine("<products>")
   for each($col in $dt.Columns)
   {
      $tstr = ""
      $tstr = "<" + $col.Caption + ">"
      $tstr = $tstr + dr[$col.Caption]
      $tstr = $tstr + "</" + $col.Caption + ">"
      $txtstream.WriteLine($tstr);
   }
   $txtstream.WriteLine("</products>")
}
$txtstream.WriteLine("</data>")
$txtstream.Close()
```

DOM CREATE ELEMENT XML

```
$ws = new-object -com WScript.Shell
$xmldoc = new-object -com MSXML2.DOMDocument();
$pi = xmldoc.CreateProcessingInstruction("xml", "version='1.0' encoding='iso-
8895-1'")
$oRoot = $xmldoc.CreateElement("data")
$xmldoc.AppendChild($pi);
foreach ($dr in $dt.Rows)
{
   $oNode = $xmldoc.CreateNode(0, "Products")
   foreach ( $col in $dt.Columns)
   {
      $oNode1 = $xmldoc.CreateNode(0, $col.Caption)
      $oNode1.innerText =$dr[$col.Caption].ToString()
```

```
        $oNode.AppendChild($oNode1)
    }
    $oRoot.AppendChild($oNode)
}
$xmldoc.AppendChild($oRoot)
$xmldoc.Save($ws.CurrentDirectory + "\\Products.xml")
```

TEXT CREATED ELEMENT XML FOR XLS

```
$ws = new-object -com WScript.Shell
$fso = new-object -com Scripting.FileSystemObject
$txtstream = $fso.OpenTextFile($ws.CurrentDirectory + "\\Products.xml", 2, $true,
-2)
$txtstream.WriteLine("<?xml version='1.0' encoding='iso-8859-1'?>")
$txtstream.WriteLine("<?xml-stylesheet type='Text/xsl' href='Products.xsl'?>")

$txtstream.WriteLine("<data>")
foreach($dr in  $dt.rows)
{
    $txtstream.WriteLine("<products>")
    for each($col in  $dt.Columns)
    {
        string $tstr = "";
        $tstr = "<" + $col.Caption + ">"
        $tstr = $tstr + $dr[$col.Caption].ToString()
        $tstr = $tstr + "</" + $col.Caption + ">"
        $txtstream.WriteLine($tstr)
    }
    $txtstream.WriteLine("</products>")
}
$txtstream.WriteLine("</data>")
$txtstream.Close()
```

DOM CREATE ELEMENT XML FOR XSL

```
$ws = new-object -com WScript.Shell
$xmldoc = new-object -com MSXML2.DOMDocument()
$pi = xmldoc.CreateProcessingInstruction("xml", "version='1.0' encoding='iso-
8895-1'")
$pii = $xmldoc.CreateProcessingInstruction("xml-stylesheet", "type='text/xsl'
href='Products.xsl'")
$oRoot = xmldoc.CreateElement("data")
$xmldoc.AppendChild($pi)
$xmldoc.AppendChild($pii)
foreach ($dr in $dt.Rows)
{
    $oNode = $xmldoc.CreateNode(0, "Products")
    foreach ( $col in $dt.Columns)
    {
      $oNode1 = $xmldoc.CreateNode(0, $col.Caption)
      $oNode1.innerText =$dr[$col.Caption].ToString()
      $oNode.AppendChild($oNode1)
    }
    $oRoot.AppendChild($oNode)
}
$xmldoc.AppendChild($oRoot)
$xmldoc.Save($ws.CurrentDirectory + "\\Products.xml")
```

TEXT CREATED SCHEMA XML

```
$ws = new-object -com WScript.Shell
$fso = new-object -com Scripting.FileSystemObject
$txtstream = $fso.OpenTextFile($ws.CurrentDirectory + "\\Products.xml", 2, $true,
-2)
$txtstream.WriteLine("<?xml version=" + '"' + "1.0=" + '"' + " encoding='iso-
8859-1'?>")
$txtstream.WriteLine("<data>")
foreach($dr in $dt.rows)
{
```

```
  $txtstream.WriteLine("<products>")
  for each($col in  $dt.Columns)
  {
     string $tstr = ""
     $tstr = "<" + $col.Caption + ">"
     $tstr = $tstr + dr[$col.Caption]
     $tstr = $tstr + "</" + $col.Caption + ">"
     $txtstream.WriteLine($tstr)
  }
  $txtstream.WriteLine("</products>")
}
$txtstream.WriteLine("</data>")
$txtstream.Close()

ADODB.Recordset^ rs = gcnew ADODB.Recordset();
rs.ActiveConnection = "Provider=MSDAOSP; Data Source = MSXML2.DSOControl; ";
rs.Open(Application.StartupPath + "\\Products.xml")
rs.Save(Application.StartupPath + "\\ProductsSchema.xml")
```

DOM CREATED SCHEMA XML

```
$ws = new-object -com WScript.Shell
$xmldoc = new-object -com MSXML2.DOMDocument();
$pi = xmldoc.CreateProcessingInstruction("xml", "version='1.0' encoding='iso-
8895-1'")
$oRoot = $xmldoc.CreateElement("data")
$xmldoc.AppendChild($pi);
foreach ($dr in  $dt.Rows)
{
  $oNode = $xmldoc.CreateNode(0, "Products")
  foreach ( $col in  $dt.Columns)
  {
    $oNode1 = $xmldoc.CreateNode(0, $col.Caption)
    $oNode1.innerText =$dr[$col.Caption].ToString()
    $oNode.AppendChild($oNode1)
  }
  $oRoot.AppendChild($oNode)
}
$xmldoc.AppendChild($oRoot)
```

```
$xmldoc.Save($ws.CurrentDirectory + "\\Products.xml")

$rs = new-object -com ADODB.Recordset
$rs.ActiveConnection = "Provider=MSDAOSP; Data Source = MSXML2.DSOControl; "
$rs.Open($ws.CurrentDirectory + "\\Products.xml")
$rs.Save($ws.CurrentDirectory + "\\ProductsSchema.xml")
```

XSL FILES

BELOW ARE EXAMPLES OF WHAT YOU CAN DO WITH XSL. Views include reports and tables and orientation is for multi-line horizontal, multi-line VERTICAL, single line horizontal and single line VERTICAL.

```
$ws = new-object -com WScript.Shell
$fso = new-object -com Scripting.FileSystemObject
$txtstream = $fso.OpenTextFile($ws.CurrentDirectory + "\\Products.xsl", 2, $true, -2)
    $txtstream.WriteLine("<?xml version='1.0' encoding='UTF-8'?>")
    $txtstream.WriteLine("<xsl:stylesheet version='1.0'
xmlns:xsl='http://www.w3.org/1999/XSL/Transform'>")
    $txtstream.WriteLine("<xsl:template match='/'>")
    $txtstream.WriteLine("<html>")
    $txtstream.WriteLine("<head>")
    $txtstream.WriteLine("<title>Products</title>")
    $txtstream.WriteLine("</head>")
    $txtstream.WriteLine("<body>")
```

For Reports:

```
    $txtstream.WriteLine("<table border='0' colspacing='3' colpadding='3'>")
```

For Tables:

```
    $txtstream.WriteLine("<table border='1' colspacing='3' colpadding='3'>")
```

Single Line Horizontal

```
$txtstream.WriteLine("<tr>")
for each($col in  $dt.Columns)
{
    $txtstream.WriteLine("<th align='left' nowrap='true'>" + $col.Caption +
"</th>")
}
$txtstream.WriteLine("</tr>")
```

None

```
$txtstream.WriteLine("<tr>")
for each($col in  $dt.Columns)
{
    $txtstream.WriteLine("<td><xsl:value-of select='data/Products/" +
$col.Caption  + "'/></td>")
}
$txtstream.WriteLine("</tr>")
```

Button

```
$txtstream.WriteLine("<tr>")
for each($col in  $dt.Columns)
{
    $txtstream.WriteLine("<td  align='left' nowrap='true'><button
style='width:100%;'><xsl:value-of select='data/Products/" + $col.Caption  +
"'/></button></td>")
}
$txtstream.WriteLine("</tr>")
```

Combobox

```
$txtstream.WriteLine("<tr>")
for each($col in  $dt.Columns)
{
    $txtstream.WriteLine("<td                              align='left'
nowrap='true'><select><option><xsl:attribute           name='value'><xsl:value-of
select='data/Products/"    +    $col.Caption    +    "'/></xsl:attribute><xsl:value-of
select='data/Products/" + $col.Caption  + "'/></option></select></td>")
}
```

```
$txtstream.WriteLine("</tr>")
```

```
$txtstream.WriteLine("<tr>")
for each($col in $dt.Columns)
{
    $txtstream.WriteLine("<td     align='left'  nowrap='true'><div><xsl:value-of
select='data/Products/" + $col.Caption + "'/></div></td>")
}
$txtstream.WriteLine("</tr>")
```

```
$txtstream.WriteLine("<tr>")
for each($col in $dt.Columns)
{
    $txtstream.WriteLine("<td     align='left'   nowrap='true'><a     href='"   +
$dr[$col.Caption].ToString()    +    "'><xsl:value-of    select='data/Products/"    +
$col.Caption + "'/></a></td>")
}
$txtstream.WriteLine("</tr>")
```

```
$txtstream.WriteLine("<tr>")
for each($col in $dt.Columns)
{
    $txtstream.WriteLine("<td             align='left'        nowrap='true'><select
multiple><option><xsl:attribute                        name='value'><xsl:value-of
select='data/Products/"   +   $col.Caption    +   "'/></xsl:attribute><xsl:value-of
select='data/Products/" + $col.Caption + "'/></option></select></td>")
}
$txtstream.WriteLine("</tr>")
```

```
$txtstream.WriteLine("<tr>")
for each($col in $dt.Columns)
{
```

```
$txtstream.WriteLine("<td      align='left'  nowrap='true'><span><xsl:value-of
select='data/Products/" + $col.Caption  + "'/></span></td>")
  }
  $txtstream.WriteLine("</tr>")
```

textarea

```
  $txtstream.WriteLine("<tr>")
  for each($col in  $dt.Columns)
  {
    $txtstream.WriteLine("<td  align='left' nowrap='true'><textarea><xsl:value-of
select='data/Products/" + $col.Caption  + "'/></textarea></td>")
  }
  $txtstream.WriteLine("</tr>")
```

Textbox

```
  $txtstream.WriteLine("<tr>")
  for each($col in  $dt.Columns)
  {
    $txtstream.WriteLine("<td  align='left' nowrap='true'><input
type='text'><xsl:attribute name='value'><xsl:value-of select='data/Products/" +
$col.Caption  + "'/></xsl:attribute></input></td>")
  }
  $txtstream.WriteLine("</tr>")
```

End code for each routine:

```
  $txtstream.WriteLine("</table>")
  $txtstream.WriteLine("</body>")
  $txtstream.WriteLine("</html>")
  $txtstream.WriteLine("</xsl:template>")
  $txtstream.WriteLine("</xsl:stylesheet>")
  $txtstream.Close()
```

Multi Line Horizontal

```
$txtstream.WriteLine("<tr>")
for each($col in  $dt.Columns)
{
   $txtstream.WriteLine("<th align='left' nowrap='true'>" + $col.Caption +
"</th>")
}
$txtstream.WriteLine("</tr>")
```

None

```
$txtstream.WriteLine("<xsl:for-each select='data/products'>")
$txtstream.WriteLine("<tr>")
for each($col in  $dt.Columns)
{
   $txtstream.WriteLine("<td><xsl:value-of select=\' + $col.Caption +
"\'/></td>")
}
$txtstream.WriteLine("</tr>")
$txtstream.WriteLine("</xsl:for-each>")
```

Button

```
$txtstream.WriteLine("<xsl:for-each select='data/products'>")
$txtstream.WriteLine("<tr>")
for each($col in  $dt.Columns)
{
   $txtstream.WriteLine("<td  align='left' nowrap='true'><button
style='width:100%;'><xsl:value-of select=\' + $col.Caption  + "'/></button></td>")
}
$txtstream.WriteLine("</tr>")
$txtstream.WriteLine("</xsl:for-each>")
```

Combobox

```
$txtstream.WriteLine("<xsl:for-each select='data/products'>")
$txtstream.WriteLine("<tr>")
for each($col in  $dt.Columns)
{
   $txtstream.WriteLine("<td                                      align='left'
nowrap='true'><select><option><xsl:attribute name='value'><xsl:value-of select=\'
```

```
+  $col.Caption  +  '"/></xsl:attribute><xsl:value-of  select=\'  +  $col.Caption  +
"'/></option></select></td>")
  }
  $txtstream.WriteLine("</tr>")
  $txtstream.WriteLine("</xsl:for-each>")
```

Div

```
  $txtstream.WriteLine("<xsl:for-each select='data/products'>")
  $txtstream.WriteLine("<tr>")
  for each($col in  $dt.Columns)
  {
    $txtstream.WriteLine("<td        align='left'   nowrap='true'><div><xsl:value-of
select=\' + $col.Caption + "'/></div></td>")
  }
  $txtstream.WriteLine("</tr>")
  $txtstream.WriteLine("</xsl:for-each>")
```

Link

```
  $txtstream.WriteLine("<xsl:for-each select='data/products'>")
  $txtstream.WriteLine("<tr>")
  for each($col in  $dt.Columns)
  {
    $txtstream.WriteLine("<td        align='left'   nowrap='true'><a    href='"   +
$dr[$col.Caption].ToString()  +  "'><xsl:value-of  select=\'  +  $col.Caption  +
"'/></a></td>")
  }
  $txtstream.WriteLine("</tr>")
  $txtstream.WriteLine("</xsl:for-each>")
```

Listbox

```
  $txtstream.WriteLine("<xsl:for-each select='data/products'>")
  $txtstream.WriteLine("<tr>")
  for each($col in  $dt.Columns)
  {
    $txtstream.WriteLine("<td             align='left'        nowrap='true'><select
multiple><option><xsl:attribute      name='value'><xsl:value-of      select=\'    +
$col.Caption   +   "'/></xsl:attribute><xsl:value-of  select=\'  +  $col.Caption  +
"'/></option></select></td>")
  }
  $txtstream.WriteLine("</tr>")
```

Span

```
$txtstream.WriteLine("<xsl:for-each select='data/products'>")
$txtstream.WriteLine("<tr>")
for each($col in  $dt.Columns)
{
    $txtstream.WriteLine("<td     align='left'  nowrap='true'><span><xsl:value-of
select=\' + $col.Caption  + "'/></span></td>")
}
$txtstream.WriteLine("</tr>")
$txtstream.WriteLine("</xsl:for-each>")
```

textarea

```
$txtstream.WriteLine("<xsl:for-each select='data/products'>")
$txtstream.WriteLine("<tr>")
for each($col in  $dt.Columns)
{
    $txtstream.WriteLine("<td  align='left' nowrap='true'><textarea><xsl:value-of
select=\' + $col.Caption  + "'/></textarea></td>")
}
$txtstream.WriteLine("</tr>")
$txtstream.WriteLine("</xsl:for-each>")
```

Textbox

```
$txtstream.WriteLine("<xsl:for-each select='data/products'>")
$txtstream.WriteLine("<tr>")
for each($col in  $dt.Columns)
{
    $txtstream.WriteLine("<td  align='left' nowrap='true'><input
type='text'><xsl:attribute name='value'><xsl:value-of select=\' + $col.Caption  +
"'/></xsl:attribute></input></td>")
}
$txtstream.WriteLine("</tr>")
$txtstream.WriteLine("</xsl:for-each>")
```

End Code for Each routine.

```
$txtstream.WriteLine("</table>")
$txtstream.WriteLine("</body>")
$txtstream.WriteLine("</html>")
```

```
$txtstream.WriteLine("</xsl:template>")
$txtstream.WriteLine("</xsl:stylesheet>")
$txtstream.Close()
```

Single Line VERTICAL

```
for each($col in $dt.Columns)
{
    $txtstream.WriteLine("<tr><th align='left' nowrap='true'>" + $col.Caption +
"</th>")
```

None

```
    $txtstream.WriteLine("<td><xsl:value-of select='data/Products/" +
$col.Caption  + "'/></td></tr>")
```
Button

```
    $txtstream.WriteLine("<td align='left' nowrap='true'><button
style='width:100%;'><xsl:value-of select='data/Products/" + $col.Caption +
"'/></button></td></tr>")
```

Combobox

```
    $txtstream.WriteLine("<td                                    align='left'
nowrap='true'><select><option><xsl:attribute          name='value'><xsl:value-of
select='data/Products/"   +   $col.Caption    +   "'/></xsl:attribute><xsl:value-of
select='data/Products/" + $col.Caption + "'/></option></select></td></tr>")
```

Div

```
    $txtstream.WriteLine("<td       align='left'   nowrap='true'><div><xsl:value-of
select='data/Products/" + $col.Caption + "'/></div></td></tr>")
```
Link

```
    $txtstream.WriteLine("<td        align='left'   nowrap='true'><a   href='"   +
$dr[$col.Caption].ToString()    +    "'><xsl:value-of    select='data/Products/"    +
$col.Caption + "'/></a></td></tr>")
```
Listbox

```
$txtstream.WriteLine("<td                align='left'        nowrap='true'><select
multiple><option><xsl:attribute                    name='value'><xsl:value-of
select='data/Products/"    +    $col.Caption    +    "'/></xsl:attribute><xsl:value-of
select='data/Products/" + $col.Caption  + "'/></option></select></td></tr>")
```

```
$txtstream.WriteLine("<td     align='left'  nowrap='true'><span><xsl:value-of
select='data/Products/" + $col.Caption  + "'/></span></td></tr>")
```

```
$txtstream.WriteLine("<td  align='left' nowrap='true'><textarea><xsl:value-of
select='data/Products/" + $col.Caption  + "'/></textarea></td></tr>")
```

```
$txtstream.WriteLine("<td  align='left' nowrap='true'><input
type='text'><xsl:attribute name='value'><xsl:value-of select='data/Products/" +
$col.Caption  + "'/></xsl:attribute></input></td></tr>")
```

End Code for Each routine.

```
  }
  $txtstream.WriteLine("</table>")
  $txtstream.WriteLine("</body>")
  $txtstream.WriteLine("</html>")
  $txtstream.WriteLine("</xsl:template>")
  $txtstream.WriteLine("</xsl:stylesheet>")
  $txtstream.Close()
```

Multi Line VERTICAL

```
  for each($col in  $dt.Columns)
  {
    $txtstream.WriteLine("<tr><th align='left' nowrap='true'>" + $col.Caption +
"</th>")
```

```
$txtstream.WriteLine("<xsl:for-each select='data/products'>")
for each($col in $dt.Columns)
{
    $txtstream.WriteLine("<td><xsl:value-of select=\' + $col.Caption +
"\'/></td>")
}
$txtstream.WriteLine("</xsl:for-each>")
$txtstream.WriteLine("</tr>")
```

Button

```
$txtstream.WriteLine("<xsl:for-each select='data/products'>")
for each($col in $dt.Columns)
{
    $txtstream.WriteLine("<td align='left' nowrap='true'> <button
style='width:100%;'><xsl:value-of select=\' + $col.Caption + "'/></button></td>")
}
$txtstream.WriteLine("</tr>")
$txtstream.WriteLine("</xsl:for-each>")
```

Combobox

```
$txtstream.WriteLine("<xsl:for-each select='data/products'>")
for each($col in $dt.Columns)
{
    $txtstream.WriteLine("<td                               align='left'
nowrap='true'><select><option><xsl:attribute name='value'><xsl:value-of select=\'
+ $col.Caption   + '"/></xsl:attribute><xsl:value-of select=\' + $col.Caption   +
"'/></option></select></td>")
}
$txtstream.WriteLine("</tr>")
$txtstream.WriteLine("</xsl:for-each>")
```

Div

```
$txtstream.WriteLine("<xsl:for-each select='data/products'>")
for each($col in $dt.Columns)
{
    $txtstream.WriteLine("<td       align='left'   nowrap='true'><div><xsl:value-of
select=\' + $col.Caption + "'/></div></td>")
}
```

```
$txtstream.WriteLine("</xsl:for-each>")
$txtstream.WriteLine("</tr>")
```

Link

```
$txtstream.WriteLine("<xsl:for-each select='data/products'>")
for each($col in  $dt.Columns)
{
    $txtstream.WriteLine("<td         align='left'  nowrap='true'><a    href='"   +
$dr[$col.Caption].ToString()   +   "'><xsl:value-of   select=\'  +  $col.Caption   +
"'/></a></td>")
}
$txtstream.WriteLine("</tr>")
$txtstream.WriteLine("</xsl:for-each>")
```

Listbox

```
$txtstream.WriteLine("<xsl:for-each select='data/products'>")
for each($col in  $dt.Columns)
{
    $txtstream.WriteLine("<td              align='left'         nowrap='true'><select
multiple><option><xsl:attribute      name='value'><xsl:value-of      select=\'     +
$col.Caption   +   "'/></xsl:attribute><xsl:value-of  select=\'  +  $col.Caption   +
"'/></option></select></td>")
}
$txtstream.WriteLine("</xsl:for-each>")
$txtstream.WriteLine("</tr>")
```

Span

```
$txtstream.WriteLine("<xsl:for-each select='data/products'>")
for each($col in  $dt.Columns)
{
    $txtstream.WriteLine("<td    align='left'  nowrap='true'><span><xsl:value-of
select=\' + $col.Caption  + "'/></span></td>")
}
$txtstream.WriteLine("</xsl:for-each>")
$txtstream.WriteLine("</tr>")
```

textarea

```
$txtstream.WriteLine("<xsl:for-each select='data/products'>")
for each($col in  $dt.Columns)
{
```

```
$txtstream.WriteLine("<td align='left' nowrap='true'><textarea><xsl:value-of
select=\' + $col.Caption + "'/></textarea></td>")
    }
  $txtstream.WriteLine("</xsl:for-each>")
  $txtstream.WriteLine("</tr>")
```

Textbox

```
  $txtstream.WriteLine("<xsl:for-each select='data/products'>")

  for each($col in $dt.Columns)
  {
    $txtstream.WriteLine("<td align='left' nowrap='true'><input
type='text'><xsl:attribute name='value'><xsl:value-of select=\' + $col.Caption +
"'/></xsl:attribute></input></td>")
  }
  $txtstream.WriteLine("</xsl:for-each>")
  $txtstream.WriteLine("</tr>")
```

End Code for Each routine.

```
  $txtstream.WriteLine("</table>")
  $txtstream.WriteLine("</body>")
  $txtstream.WriteLine("</html>")
  $txtstream.WriteLine("</xsl:template>")
  $txtstream.WriteLine("</xsl:stylesheet>")
  $txtstream.Close()
```

STYLESHEETS

Fuel for Thought

T HESE ARE SUPPLIED AS IS AND ARE JUST SOME IDEAS I THINK YOU WILL LIKE. DON'T SHOOT THE MESSANGER.

None

```
$txtstream.WriteLine("<style type='text/css'>")
$txtstream.WriteLine("th")
$txtstream.WriteLine("{")
$txtstream.WriteLine("   COLOR: white;")
$txtstream.WriteLine("}")
$txtstream.WriteLine("td")
$txtstream.WriteLine("{")
$txtstream.WriteLine("   COLOR: white;")
$txtstream.WriteLine("}")
$txtstream.WriteLine("</style>")
```

Its A Table

```
$txtstream.WriteLine("<style type='text/css'>")
$txtstream.WriteLine("#itsthetable {")
$txtstream.WriteLine("   font-family: Georgia, ''Times New Roman'', Times, serif;")
$txtstream.WriteLine("   color: #036;")
$txtstream.WriteLine("}")
```

```
$txtstream.WriteLine("caption {")
$txtstream.WriteLine("    font-size: 48px;")
$txtstream.WriteLine("    color: #036;")
$txtstream.WriteLine("    font-weight: bolder;")
$txtstream.WriteLine("    font-variant: small-caps;")
$txtstream.WriteLine("}")

$txtstream.WriteLine("th {")
$txtstream.WriteLine("    font-size: 12px;")
$txtstream.WriteLine("    color: #FFF;")
$txtstream.WriteLine("    background-color: #06C;")
$txtstream.WriteLine("    padding: 8px 4px;")
$txtstream.WriteLine("    border-bottom: 1px solid #015ebc;")
$txtstream.WriteLine("}")

$txtstream.WriteLine("table {")
$txtstream.WriteLine("    margin: 0;")
$txtstream.WriteLine("    padding: 0;")
$txtstream.WriteLine("    border-collapse: collapse;")
$txtstream.WriteLine("    border: 1px solid #06C;")
$txtstream.WriteLine("    width: 100%")
$txtstream.WriteLine("}")

$txtstream.WriteLine("#itsthetable th a:link, #itsthetable th a:visited {")
$txtstream.WriteLine("    color: #FFF;")
$txtstream.WriteLine("    text-decoration: none;")
$txtstream.WriteLine("    border-left: 5px solid #FFF;")
$txtstream.WriteLine("    padding-left: 3px;")
$txtstream.WriteLine("}")

$txtstream.WriteLine("th a:hover, #itsthetable th a:active {")
$txtstream.WriteLine("    color: #F90;")
$txtstream.WriteLine("    text-decoration: line-through;")
$txtstream.WriteLine("    border-left: 5px solid #F90;")
$txtstream.WriteLine("    padding-left: 3px;")
$txtstream.WriteLine("}")

$txtstream.WriteLine("tbody th:hover {")
$txtstream.WriteLine("    background-image: url(imgs/tbody_hover.gif);")
$txtstream.WriteLine("    background-position: bottom;")
$txtstream.WriteLine("    background-repeat: repeat-x;")
$txtstream.WriteLine("}")

$txtstream.WriteLine("td {")
$txtstream.WriteLine("    background-color: #f2f2f2;")
$txtstream.WriteLine("    padding: 4px;")
$txtstream.WriteLine("    font-size: 12px;")
$txtstream.WriteLine("}")

$txtstream.WriteLine("#itsthetable td:hover {")
```

```
$txtstream.WriteLine("    background-color: #f8f8f8;")

$txtstream.WriteLine("}")

$txtstream.WriteLine("#itsthetable td a:link, #itsthetable td a:visited {")
$txtstream.WriteLine("    color: #039;")
$txtstream.WriteLine("    text-decoration: none;")
$txtstream.WriteLine("    border-left: 3px solid #039;")
$txtstream.WriteLine("    padding-left: 3px;")
$txtstream.WriteLine("}")

$txtstream.WriteLine("#itsthetable td a:hover, #itsthetable td a:active {")
$txtstream.WriteLine("    color: #06C;")
$txtstream.WriteLine("    text-decoration: line-through;")
$txtstream.WriteLine("    border-left: 3px solid #06C;")
$txtstream.WriteLine("    padding-left: 3px;")
$txtstream.WriteLine("}")

$txtstream.WriteLine("#itsthetable th {")
$txtstream.WriteLine("    text-align: left;")
$txtstream.WriteLine("    width: 150px;")
$txtstream.WriteLine("}")

$txtstream.WriteLine("#itsthetable tr {")
$txtstream.WriteLine("    border-bottom: 1px solid #CCC;")
$txtstream.WriteLine("}")

$txtstream.WriteLine("#itsthetable thead th {")
$txtstream.WriteLine("    background-image: url(imgs/thead_back.gif);")
$txtstream.WriteLine("    background-repeat: repeat-x;")
$txtstream.WriteLine("    background-color: #06C;")
$txtstream.WriteLine("    height: 30px;")
$txtstream.WriteLine("    font-size: 18px;")
$txtstream.WriteLine("    text-align: center;")
$txtstream.WriteLine("    text-shadow: #333 2px 2px;")
$txtstream.WriteLine("    border: 2px;")
$txtstream.WriteLine("}")

$txtstream.WriteLine("#itsthetable tfoot th {")
$txtstream.WriteLine("    background-image: url(imgs/tfoot_back.gif);")
$txtstream.WriteLine("    background-repeat: repeat-x;")
$txtstream.WriteLine("    background-color: #036;")
$txtstream.WriteLine("    height: 30px;")
$txtstream.WriteLine("    font-size: 28px;")
$txtstream.WriteLine("    text-align: center;")
$txtstream.WriteLine("    text-shadow: #333 2px 2px;")
$txtstream.WriteLine("}")

$txtstream.WriteLine("#itsthetable tfoot td {")
$txtstream.WriteLine("    background-image: url(imgs/tfoot_back.gif);")
```

```
$txtstream.WriteLine("    background-repeat: repeat-x;")
$txtstream.WriteLine("    background-color: #036;")
$txtstream.WriteLine("    color: FFF;")
$txtstream.WriteLine("    height: 30px;")
$txtstream.WriteLine("    font-size: 24px;")
$txtstream.WriteLine("    text-align: left;")
$txtstream.WriteLine("    text-shadow: #333 2px 2px;")
$txtstream.WriteLine("}")

$txtstream.WriteLine("tbody td a[href=''http://www.csslab.cl/''] {")
$txtstream.WriteLine("    font-weight: bolder;")
$txtstream.WriteLine("}")
$txtstream.WriteLine("</style>")
```

Black and White Text

```
$txtstream.WriteLine("<style type='text/css'>")
$txtstream.WriteLine("th")
$txtstream.WriteLine("{")
$txtstream.WriteLine("    COLOR: white;")
$txtstream.WriteLine("    BACKGROUND-COLOR: black;")
$txtstream.WriteLine("    FONT-FAMILY: Cambria, serif;")
$txtstream.WriteLine("    FONT-SIZE: 12px;")
$txtstream.WriteLine("    text-align: left;")
$txtstream.WriteLine("    white-Space: nowrap='nowrap';")
$txtstream.WriteLine("}")
$txtstream.WriteLine("td")
$txtstream.WriteLine("{")
$txtstream.WriteLine("    COLOR: white;")
$txtstream.WriteLine("    BACKGROUND-COLOR: black;")
$txtstream.WriteLine("    FONT-FAMILY: Cambria, serif;")
$txtstream.WriteLine("    FONT-SIZE: 12px;")
$txtstream.WriteLine("    text-align: left;")
$txtstream.WriteLine("    white-Space: nowrap='nowrap';")
$txtstream.WriteLine("}")
$txtstream.WriteLine("div")
$txtstream.WriteLine("{")
$txtstream.WriteLine("    COLOR: white;")
$txtstream.WriteLine("    BACKGROUND-COLOR: black;")
$txtstream.WriteLine("    FONT-FAMILY: Cambria, serif;")
$txtstream.WriteLine("    FONT-SIZE: 10px;")
$txtstream.WriteLine("    text-align: left;")
$txtstream.WriteLine("    white-Space: nowrap='nowrap';")
$txtstream.WriteLine("}")
$txtstream.WriteLine("span")
$txtstream.WriteLine("{")
$txtstream.WriteLine("    COLOR: white;")
$txtstream.WriteLine("    BACKGROUND-COLOR: black;")
```

```
$txtstream.WriteLine("    FONT-FAMILY:  Cambria, serif;")
$txtstream.WriteLine("    FONT-SIZE: 10px;")
$txtstream.WriteLine("    text-align: left;")
$txtstream.WriteLine("    white-Space: nowrap='nowrap';")
$txtstream.WriteLine("    display:inline-block;")
$txtstream.WriteLine("    width: 100%;")
$txtstream.WriteLine("}")
$txtstream.WriteLine("textarea")
$txtstream.WriteLine("{")
$txtstream.WriteLine("    COLOR: white;")
$txtstream.WriteLine("    BACKGROUND-COLOR: black;")
$txtstream.WriteLine("    FONT-FAMILY:  Cambria, serif;")
$txtstream.WriteLine("    FONT-SIZE: 10px;")
$txtstream.WriteLine("    text-align: left;")
$txtstream.WriteLine("    white-Space: nowrap='nowrap';")
$txtstream.WriteLine("    width: 100%;")
$txtstream.WriteLine("}")
$txtstream.WriteLine("select")
$txtstream.WriteLine("{")
$txtstream.WriteLine("    COLOR: white;")
$txtstream.WriteLine("    BACKGROUND-COLOR: black;")
$txtstream.WriteLine("    FONT-FAMILY:  Cambria, serif;")
$txtstream.WriteLine("    FONT-SIZE: 10px;")
$txtstream.WriteLine("    text-align: left;")
$txtstream.WriteLine("    white-Space: nowrap='nowrap';")
$txtstream.WriteLine("    width: 100%;")
$txtstream.WriteLine("}")
$txtstream.WriteLine("input")
$txtstream.WriteLine("{")
$txtstream.WriteLine("    COLOR: white;")
$txtstream.WriteLine("    BACKGROUND-COLOR: black;")
$txtstream.WriteLine("    FONT-FAMILY:  Cambria, serif;")
$txtstream.WriteLine("    FONT-SIZE: 12px;")
$txtstream.WriteLine("    text-align: left;")
$txtstream.WriteLine("    display:table-cell;")
$txtstream.WriteLine("    white-Space: nowrap='nowrap';")
$txtstream.WriteLine("}")
$txtstream.WriteLine("h1 {")
$txtstream.WriteLine("color: antiquewhite;")
$txtstream.WriteLine("text-shadow: 1px 1px 1px black;")
$txtstream.WriteLine("padding: 3px;")
$txtstream.WriteLine("text-align: center;")
$txtstream.WriteLine("box-shadow: inset 2px 2px 5px rgba(0,0,0,0.5), inset -2px -
2px 5px rgba(255,255,255,0.5);")
$txtstream.WriteLine("}")
$txtstream.WriteLine("</style>")
```

Colored Text

```
$txtstream.WriteLine("<style type='text/css'>")
$txtstream.WriteLine("th")
$txtstream.WriteLine("{")
$txtstream.WriteLine("   COLOR: darkred;")
$txtstream.WriteLine("   BACKGROUND-COLOR: #eeeeee;")
$txtstream.WriteLine("   FONT-FAMILY: Cambria, serif;")
$txtstream.WriteLine("   FONT-SIZE: 12px;")
$txtstream.WriteLine("   text-align: left;")
$txtstream.WriteLine("   white-Space: nowrap='nowrap';")
$txtstream.WriteLine("}")
$txtstream.WriteLine("td")
$txtstream.WriteLine("{")
$txtstream.WriteLine("   COLOR: navy;")
$txtstream.WriteLine("   BACKGROUND-COLOR: #eeeeee;")
$txtstream.WriteLine("   FONT-FAMILY: Cambria, serif;")
$txtstream.WriteLine("   FONT-SIZE: 12px;")
$txtstream.WriteLine("   text-align: left;")
$txtstream.WriteLine("   white-Space: nowrap='nowrap';")
$txtstream.WriteLine("}")
$txtstream.WriteLine("div")
$txtstream.WriteLine("{")
$txtstream.WriteLine("   COLOR: white;")
$txtstream.WriteLine("   BACKGROUND-COLOR: navy;")
$txtstream.WriteLine("   FONT-FAMILY: Cambria, serif;")
$txtstream.WriteLine("   FONT-SIZE: 10px;")
$txtstream.WriteLine("   text-align: left;")
$txtstream.WriteLine("   white-Space: nowrap='nowrap';")
$txtstream.WriteLine("}")
$txtstream.WriteLine("span")
$txtstream.WriteLine("{")
$txtstream.WriteLine("   COLOR: white;")
$txtstream.WriteLine("   BACKGROUND-COLOR: navy;")
$txtstream.WriteLine("   FONT-FAMILY: Cambria, serif;")
$txtstream.WriteLine("   FONT-SIZE: 10px;")
$txtstream.WriteLine("   text-align: left;")
$txtstream.WriteLine("   white-Space: nowrap='nowrap';")
$txtstream.WriteLine("   display:inline-block;")
$txtstream.WriteLine("   width: 100%;")
$txtstream.WriteLine("}")
$txtstream.WriteLine("textarea")
$txtstream.WriteLine("{")
$txtstream.WriteLine("   COLOR: white;")
$txtstream.WriteLine("   BACKGROUND-COLOR: navy;")
$txtstream.WriteLine("   FONT-FAMILY: Cambria, serif;")
$txtstream.WriteLine("   FONT-SIZE: 10px;")
$txtstream.WriteLine("   text-align: left;")
```

```
$txtstream.WriteLine("    white-Space: nowrap='nowrap';")
$txtstream.WriteLine("    width: 100%;")
$txtstream.WriteLine("}")
$txtstream.WriteLine("select")
$txtstream.WriteLine("{")
$txtstream.WriteLine("    COLOR: white;")
$txtstream.WriteLine("    BACKGROUND-COLOR: navy;")
$txtstream.WriteLine("    FONT-FAMILY:  Cambria, serif;")
$txtstream.WriteLine("    FONT-SIZE: 10px;")
$txtstream.WriteLine("    text-align: left;")
$txtstream.WriteLine("    white-Space: nowrap='nowrap';")
$txtstream.WriteLine("    width: 100%;")
$txtstream.WriteLine("}")
$txtstream.WriteLine("input")
$txtstream.WriteLine("{")
$txtstream.WriteLine("    COLOR: white;")
$txtstream.WriteLine("    BACKGROUND-COLOR: navy;")
$txtstream.WriteLine("    FONT-FAMILY:  Cambria, serif;")
$txtstream.WriteLine("    FONT-SIZE: 12px;")
$txtstream.WriteLine("    text-align: left;")
$txtstream.WriteLine("    display:table-cell;")
$txtstream.WriteLine("    white-Space: nowrap='nowrap';")
$txtstream.WriteLine("}")
$txtstream.WriteLine("h1 {")
$txtstream.WriteLine("color: antiquewhite;")
$txtstream.WriteLine("text-shadow: 1px 1px 1px black;")
$txtstream.WriteLine("padding: 3px;")
$txtstream.WriteLine("text-align: center;")
$txtstream.WriteLine("box-shadow: inset 2px 2px 5px rgba(0,0,0,0.5), inset -2px -
2px 5px rgba(255,255,255,0.5);")
$txtstream.WriteLine("}")
$txtstream.WriteLine("</style>")
```

Oscillating Row Colors

```
$txtstream.WriteLine("<style type='text/css'>")
$txtstream.WriteLine("th")
$txtstream.WriteLine("{")
$txtstream.WriteLine("    COLOR: white;")
$txtstream.WriteLine("    BACKGROUND-COLOR: navy;")
$txtstream.WriteLine("    FONT-FAMILY: Cambria, serif;")
$txtstream.WriteLine("    FONT-SIZE: 12px;")
$txtstream.WriteLine("    text-align: left;")
$txtstream.WriteLine("    white-Space: nowrap='nowrap';")
$txtstream.WriteLine("}")
$txtstream.WriteLine("td")
$txtstream.WriteLine("{")
```

```
$txtstream.WriteLine("    COLOR: navy;")
$txtstream.WriteLine("    FONT-FAMILY: Cambria, serif;")
$txtstream.WriteLine("    FONT-SIZE: 12px;")
$txtstream.WriteLine("    text-align: left;")
$txtstream.WriteLine("    white-Space: nowrap='nowrap';")
$txtstream.WriteLine("}")
$txtstream.WriteLine("div")
$txtstream.WriteLine("{")
$txtstream.WriteLine("    COLOR: navy;")
$txtstream.WriteLine("    FONT-FAMILY: Cambria, serif;")
$txtstream.WriteLine("    FONT-SIZE: 12px;")
$txtstream.WriteLine("    text-align: left;")
$txtstream.WriteLine("    white-Space: nowrap='nowrap';")
$txtstream.WriteLine("}")
$txtstream.WriteLine("span")
$txtstream.WriteLine("{")
$txtstream.WriteLine("    COLOR: navy;")
$txtstream.WriteLine("    FONT-FAMILY: Cambria, serif;")
$txtstream.WriteLine("    FONT-SIZE: 12px;")
$txtstream.WriteLine("    text-align: left;")
$txtstream.WriteLine("    white-Space: nowrap='nowrap';")
$txtstream.WriteLine("    width: 100%;")
$txtstream.WriteLine("}")
$txtstream.WriteLine("textarea")
$txtstream.WriteLine("{")
$txtstream.WriteLine("    COLOR: navy;")
$txtstream.WriteLine("    FONT-FAMILY: Cambria, serif;")
$txtstream.WriteLine("    FONT-SIZE: 12px;")
$txtstream.WriteLine("    text-align: left;")
$txtstream.WriteLine("    white-Space: nowrap='nowrap';")
$txtstream.WriteLine("    display:inline-block;")
$txtstream.WriteLine("    width: 100%;")
$txtstream.WriteLine("}")
$txtstream.WriteLine("select")
$txtstream.WriteLine("{")
$txtstream.WriteLine("    COLOR: navy;")
$txtstream.WriteLine("    FONT-FAMILY: Cambria, serif;")
$txtstream.WriteLine("    FONT-SIZE: 10px;")
$txtstream.WriteLine("    text-align: left;")
$txtstream.WriteLine("    white-Space: nowrap='nowrap';")
$txtstream.WriteLine("    display:inline-block;")
$txtstream.WriteLine("    width: 100%;")
$txtstream.WriteLine("}")
$txtstream.WriteLine("input")
$txtstream.WriteLine("{")
$txtstream.WriteLine("    COLOR: navy;")
$txtstream.WriteLine("    FONT-FAMILY: Cambria, serif;")
$txtstream.WriteLine("    FONT-SIZE: 12px;")
$txtstream.WriteLine("    text-align: left;")
$txtstream.WriteLine("    display:table-cell;")
```

```
$txtstream.WriteLine("    white-Space: nowrap='nowrap';")
$txtstream.WriteLine("}")
$txtstream.WriteLine("h1 {")
$txtstream.WriteLine("color: antiquewhite;")
$txtstream.WriteLine("text-shadow: 1px 1px 1px black;")
$txtstream.WriteLine("padding: 3px;")
$txtstream.WriteLine("text-align: center;")
$txtstream.WriteLine("box-shadow: inset 2px 2px 5px rgba(0,0,0,0.5), inset -2px -
2px 5px rgba(255,255,255,0.5);")
$txtstream.WriteLine("}")
$txtstream.WriteLine("tr:nth-child(even){background-color:#f2f2f2;}")
$txtstream.WriteLine("tr:nth-child(odd){background-color:#cccccc;
color:#f2f2f2;}")
$txtstream.WriteLine("</style>")
```

Ghost Decorated

```
$txtstream.WriteLine("<style type='text/css'>")
$txtstream.WriteLine("th")
$txtstream.WriteLine("{")
$txtstream.WriteLine("    COLOR: black;")
$txtstream.WriteLine("    BACKGROUND-COLOR: white;")
$txtstream.WriteLine("    FONT-FAMILY: Cambria, serif;")
$txtstream.WriteLine("    FONT-SIZE: 12px;")
$txtstream.WriteLine("    text-align: left;")
$txtstream.WriteLine("    white-Space: nowrap='nowrap';")
$txtstream.WriteLine("}")
$txtstream.WriteLine("td")
$txtstream.WriteLine("{")
$txtstream.WriteLine("    COLOR: black;")
$txtstream.WriteLine("    BACKGROUND-COLOR: white;")
$txtstream.WriteLine("    FONT-FAMILY: Cambria, serif;")
$txtstream.WriteLine("    FONT-SIZE: 12px;")
$txtstream.WriteLine("    text-align: left;")
$txtstream.WriteLine("    white-Space: nowrap='nowrap';")
$txtstream.WriteLine("}")
$txtstream.WriteLine("div")
$txtstream.WriteLine("{")
$txtstream.WriteLine("    COLOR: black;")
$txtstream.WriteLine("    BACKGROUND-COLOR: white;")
$txtstream.WriteLine("    FONT-FAMILY: Cambria, serif;")
$txtstream.WriteLine("    FONT-SIZE: 10px;")
$txtstream.WriteLine("    text-align: left;")
$txtstream.WriteLine("    white-Space: nowrap='nowrap';")
$txtstream.WriteLine("}")
$txtstream.WriteLine("span")
$txtstream.WriteLine("{")
$txtstream.WriteLine("    COLOR: black;")
$txtstream.WriteLine("    BACKGROUND-COLOR: white;")
```

```
$txtstream.WriteLine("    FONT-FAMILY:  Cambria, serif;")
$txtstream.WriteLine("    FONT-SIZE: 10px;")
$txtstream.WriteLine("    text-align: left;")
$txtstream.WriteLine("    white-Space: nowrap='nowrap';")
$txtstream.WriteLine("    display:inline-block;")
$txtstream.WriteLine("    width: 100%;")
$txtstream.WriteLine("}")
$txtstream.WriteLine("textarea")
$txtstream.WriteLine("{")
$txtstream.WriteLine("    COLOR: black;")
$txtstream.WriteLine("    BACKGROUND-COLOR: white;")
$txtstream.WriteLine("    FONT-FAMILY:  Cambria, serif;")
$txtstream.WriteLine("    FONT-SIZE: 10px;")
$txtstream.WriteLine("    text-align: left;")
$txtstream.WriteLine("    white-Space: nowrap='nowrap';")
$txtstream.WriteLine("    width: 100%;")
$txtstream.WriteLine("}")
$txtstream.WriteLine("select")
$txtstream.WriteLine("{")
$txtstream.WriteLine("    COLOR: black;")
$txtstream.WriteLine("    BACKGROUND-COLOR: white;")
$txtstream.WriteLine("    FONT-FAMILY:  Cambria, serif;")
$txtstream.WriteLine("    FONT-SIZE: 10px;")
$txtstream.WriteLine("    text-align: left;")
$txtstream.WriteLine("    white-Space: nowrap='nowrap';")
$txtstream.WriteLine("    width: 100%;")
$txtstream.WriteLine("}")
$txtstream.WriteLine("input")
$txtstream.WriteLine("{")
$txtstream.WriteLine("    COLOR: black;")
$txtstream.WriteLine("    BACKGROUND-COLOR: white;")
$txtstream.WriteLine("    FONT-FAMILY:  Cambria, serif;")
$txtstream.WriteLine("    FONT-SIZE: 12px;")
$txtstream.WriteLine("    text-align: left;")
$txtstream.WriteLine("    display:table-cell;")
$txtstream.WriteLine("    white-Space: nowrap='nowrap';")
$txtstream.WriteLine("}")
$txtstream.WriteLine("h1 {")
$txtstream.WriteLine("color: antiquewhite;")
$txtstream.WriteLine("text-shadow: 1px 1px 1px black;")
$txtstream.WriteLine("padding: 3px;")
$txtstream.WriteLine("text-align: center;")
$txtstream.WriteLine("box-shadow: inset 2px 2px 5px rgba(0,0,0,0.5), inset -2px -
2px 5px rgba(255,255,255,0.5);")
$txtstream.WriteLine("}")
$txtstream.WriteLine("</style>")
```

3D

```
$txtstream.WriteLine("<style type='text/css'>")
$txtstream.WriteLine("body")
$txtstream.WriteLine("{")
$txtstream.WriteLine("   PADDING-RIGHT: 0px;")
$txtstream.WriteLine("   PADDING-LEFT: 0px;")
$txtstream.WriteLine("   PADDING-BOTTOM: 0px;")
$txtstream.WriteLine("   MARGIN: 0px;")
$txtstream.WriteLine("   COLOR: #333;")
$txtstream.WriteLine("   PADDING-TOP: 0px;")
$txtstream.WriteLine("   FONT-FAMILY: verdana, arial, helvetica, sans-serif;")
$txtstream.WriteLine("}")
$txtstream.WriteLine("table")
$txtstream.WriteLine("{")
$txtstream.WriteLine("   BORDER-RIGHT: #999999 3px solid;")
$txtstream.WriteLine("   PADDING-RIGHT: 6px;")
$txtstream.WriteLine("   PADDING-LEFT: 6px;")
$txtstream.WriteLine("   FONT-WEIGHT: Bold;")
$txtstream.WriteLine("   FONT-SIZE: 14px;")
$txtstream.WriteLine("   PADDING-BOTTOM: 6px;")
$txtstream.WriteLine("   COLOR: Peru;")
$txtstream.WriteLine("   LINE-HEIGHT: 14px;")
$txtstream.WriteLine("   PADDING-TOP: 6px;")
$txtstream.WriteLine("   BORDER-BOTTOM: #999 1px solid;")
$txtstream.WriteLine("   BACKGROUND-COLOR: #eeeeee;")
$txtstream.WriteLine("   FONT-FAMILY: verdana, arial, helvetica, sans-serif;")
$txtstream.WriteLine("   FONT-SIZE: 12px;")
$txtstream.WriteLine("}")
$txtstream.WriteLine("th")
$txtstream.WriteLine("{")
$txtstream.WriteLine("   BORDER-RIGHT: #999999 3px solid;")
$txtstream.WriteLine("   PADDING-RIGHT: 6px;")
$txtstream.WriteLine("   PADDING-LEFT: 6px;")
$txtstream.WriteLine("   FONT-WEIGHT: Bold;")
$txtstream.WriteLine("   FONT-SIZE: 14px;")
$txtstream.WriteLine("   PADDING-BOTTOM: 6px;")
$txtstream.WriteLine("   COLOR: darkred;")
$txtstream.WriteLine("   LINE-HEIGHT: 14px;")
$txtstream.WriteLine("   PADDING-TOP: 6px;")
$txtstream.WriteLine("   BORDER-BOTTOM: #999 1px solid;")
$txtstream.WriteLine("   BACKGROUND-COLOR: #eeeeee;")
$txtstream.WriteLine("   FONT-FAMILY: Cambria, serif;")
$txtstream.WriteLine("   FONT-SIZE: 12px;")
$txtstream.WriteLine("   text-align: left;")
$txtstream.WriteLine("   white-Space: nowrap='nowrap';")
$txtstream.WriteLine("}")
```

```
$txtstream.WriteLine(".th")
$txtstream.WriteLine("{")
$txtstream.WriteLine("    BORDER-RIGHT: #999999 2px solid;")
$txtstream.WriteLine("    PADDING-RIGHT: 6px;")
$txtstream.WriteLine("    PADDING-LEFT: 6px;")
$txtstream.WriteLine("    FONT-WEIGHT: Bold;")
$txtstream.WriteLine("    PADDING-BOTTOM: 6px;")
$txtstream.WriteLine("    COLOR: black;")
$txtstream.WriteLine("    PADDING-TOP: 6px;")
$txtstream.WriteLine("    BORDER-BOTTOM: #999 2px solid;")
$txtstream.WriteLine("    BACKGROUND-COLOR: #eeeeee;")
$txtstream.WriteLine("    FONT-FAMILY: Cambria, serif;")
$txtstream.WriteLine("    FONT-SIZE: 10px;")
$txtstream.WriteLine("    text-align: right;")
$txtstream.WriteLine("    white-Space: nowrap='nowrap';")
$txtstream.WriteLine("}")
$txtstream.WriteLine("td")
$txtstream.WriteLine("{")
$txtstream.WriteLine("    BORDER-RIGHT: #999999 3px solid;")
$txtstream.WriteLine("    PADDING-RIGHT: 6px;")
$txtstream.WriteLine("    PADDING-LEFT: 6px;")
$txtstream.WriteLine("    FONT-WEIGHT: Normal;")
$txtstream.WriteLine("    PADDING-BOTTOM: 6px;")
$txtstream.WriteLine("    COLOR: navy;")
$txtstream.WriteLine("    LINE-HEIGHT: 14px;")
$txtstream.WriteLine("    PADDING-TOP: 6px;")
$txtstream.WriteLine("    BORDER-BOTTOM: #999 1px solid;")
$txtstream.WriteLine("    BACKGROUND-COLOR: #eeeeee;")
$txtstream.WriteLine("    FONT-FAMILY: Cambria, serif;")
$txtstream.WriteLine("    FONT-SIZE: 12px;")
$txtstream.WriteLine("    text-align: left;")
$txtstream.WriteLine("    white-Space: nowrap='nowrap';")
$txtstream.WriteLine("}")
$txtstream.WriteLine("div")
$txtstream.WriteLine("{")
$txtstream.WriteLine("    BORDER-RIGHT: #999999 3px solid;")
$txtstream.WriteLine("    PADDING-RIGHT: 6px;")
$txtstream.WriteLine("    PADDING-LEFT: 6px;")
$txtstream.WriteLine("    FONT-WEIGHT: Normal;")
$txtstream.WriteLine("    PADDING-BOTTOM: 6px;")
$txtstream.WriteLine("    COLOR: white;")
$txtstream.WriteLine("    PADDING-TOP: 6px;")
$txtstream.WriteLine("    BORDER-BOTTOM: #999 1px solid;")
$txtstream.WriteLine("    BACKGROUND-COLOR: navy;")
$txtstream.WriteLine("    FONT-FAMILY: Cambria, serif;")
$txtstream.WriteLine("    FONT-SIZE: 10px;")
$txtstream.WriteLine("    text-align: left;")
$txtstream.WriteLine("    white-Space: nowrap='nowrap';")
$txtstream.WriteLine("}")
$txtstream.WriteLine("span")
```

```
$txtstream.WriteLine("{")
$txtstream.WriteLine("    BORDER-RIGHT: #999999 3px solid;")
$txtstream.WriteLine("    PADDING-RIGHT: 3px;")
$txtstream.WriteLine("    PADDING-LEFT: 3px;")
$txtstream.WriteLine("    FONT-WEIGHT: Normal;")
$txtstream.WriteLine("    PADDING-BOTTOM: 3px;")
$txtstream.WriteLine("    COLOR: white;")
$txtstream.WriteLine("    PADDING-TOP: 3px;")
$txtstream.WriteLine("    BORDER-BOTTOM: #999 1px solid;")
$txtstream.WriteLine("    BACKGROUND-COLOR: navy;")
$txtstream.WriteLine("    FONT-FAMILY: Cambria, serif;")
$txtstream.WriteLine("    FONT-SIZE: 10px;")
$txtstream.WriteLine("    text-align: left;")
$txtstream.WriteLine("    white-Space: nowrap='nowrap';")
$txtstream.WriteLine("    display:inline-block;")
$txtstream.WriteLine("    width: 100%;")
$txtstream.WriteLine("}")
$txtstream.WriteLine("textarea")
$txtstream.WriteLine("{")
$txtstream.WriteLine("    BORDER-RIGHT: #999999 3px solid;")
$txtstream.WriteLine("    PADDING-RIGHT: 3px;")
$txtstream.WriteLine("    PADDING-LEFT: 3px;")
$txtstream.WriteLine("    FONT-WEIGHT: Normal;")
$txtstream.WriteLine("    PADDING-BOTTOM: 3px;")
$txtstream.WriteLine("    COLOR: white;")
$txtstream.WriteLine("    PADDING-TOP: 3px;")
$txtstream.WriteLine("    BORDER-BOTTOM: #999 1px solid;")
$txtstream.WriteLine("    BACKGROUND-COLOR: navy;")
$txtstream.WriteLine("    FONT-FAMILY: Cambria, serif;")
$txtstream.WriteLine("    FONT-SIZE: 10px;")
$txtstream.WriteLine("    text-align: left;")
$txtstream.WriteLine("    white-Space: nowrap='nowrap';")
$txtstream.WriteLine("    width: 100%;")
$txtstream.WriteLine("}")
$txtstream.WriteLine("select")
$txtstream.WriteLine("{")
$txtstream.WriteLine("    BORDER-RIGHT: #999999 3px solid;")
$txtstream.WriteLine("    PADDING-RIGHT: 6px;")
$txtstream.WriteLine("    PADDING-LEFT: 6px;")
$txtstream.WriteLine("    FONT-WEIGHT: Normal;")
$txtstream.WriteLine("    PADDING-BOTTOM: 6px;")
$txtstream.WriteLine("    COLOR: white;")
$txtstream.WriteLine("    PADDING-TOP: 6px;")
$txtstream.WriteLine("    BORDER-BOTTOM: #999 1px solid;")
$txtstream.WriteLine("    BACKGROUND-COLOR: navy;")
$txtstream.WriteLine("    FONT-FAMILY: Cambria, serif;")
$txtstream.WriteLine("    FONT-SIZE: 10px;")
$txtstream.WriteLine("    text-align: left;")
$txtstream.WriteLine("    white-Space: nowrap='nowrap';")
$txtstream.WriteLine("    width: 100%;")
```

```
$txtstream.WriteLine("}")
$txtstream.WriteLine("input")
$txtstream.WriteLine("{")
$txtstream.WriteLine("    BORDER-RIGHT: #999999 3px solid;")
$txtstream.WriteLine("    PADDING-RIGHT: 3px;")
$txtstream.WriteLine("    PADDING-LEFT: 3px;")
$txtstream.WriteLine("    FONT-WEIGHT: Bold;")
$txtstream.WriteLine("    PADDING-BOTTOM: 3px;")
$txtstream.WriteLine("    COLOR: white;")
$txtstream.WriteLine("    PADDING-TOP: 3px;")
$txtstream.WriteLine("    BORDER-BOTTOM: #999 1px solid;")
$txtstream.WriteLine("    BACKGROUND-COLOR: navy;")
$txtstream.WriteLine("    FONT-FAMILY:  Cambria, serif;")
$txtstream.WriteLine("    FONT-SIZE: 12px;")
$txtstream.WriteLine("    text-align: left;")
$txtstream.WriteLine("    display:table-cell;")
$txtstream.WriteLine("    white-Space: nowrap='nowrap';")
$txtstream.WriteLine("    width: 100%,")
$txtstream.WriteLine("}")
$txtstream.WriteLine("h1 {")
$txtstream.WriteLine("color: antiquewhite;")
$txtstream.WriteLine("text-shadow: 1px 1px 1px black;")
$txtstream.WriteLine("padding: 3px;")
$txtstream.WriteLine("text-align: center;")
$txtstream.WriteLine("box-shadow: inset 2px 2px 5px rgba(0,0,0,0.5), inset -2px -2px 5px rgba(255,255,255,0.5);")
$txtstream.WriteLine("}")
$txtstream.WriteLine("</style>")
```

Shadow Box

```
$txtstream.WriteLine("<style type='text/css'>")
$txtstream.WriteLine("body")
$txtstream.WriteLine("{")
$txtstream.WriteLine("    PADDING-RIGHT: 0px;")
$txtstream.WriteLine("    PADDING-LEFT: 0px;")
$txtstream.WriteLine("    PADDING-BOTTOM: 0px;")
$txtstream.WriteLine("    MARGIN: 0px;")
$txtstream.WriteLine("    COLOR: #333;")
$txtstream.WriteLine("    PADDING-TOP: 0px;")
$txtstream.WriteLine("    FONT-FAMILY: verdana, arial, helvetica, sans-serif;")
$txtstream.WriteLine("}")
$txtstream.WriteLine("table")
$txtstream.WriteLine("{")
$txtstream.WriteLine("    BORDER-RIGHT: #999999 1px solid;")
$txtstream.WriteLine("    PADDING-RIGHT: 1px;")
$txtstream.WriteLine("    PADDING-LEFT: 1px;")
$txtstream.WriteLine("    PADDING-BOTTOM: 1px;")
$txtstream.WriteLine("    LINE-HEIGHT: 8px;")
```

```
$txtstream.WriteLine("    PADDING-TOP: 1px;")
$txtstream.WriteLine("    BORDER-BOTTOM: #999 1px solid;")
$txtstream.WriteLine("    BACKGROUND-COLOR: #eeeeee;")
$txtstream.WriteLine("
filter:progid:DXImageTransform.Microsoft.Shadow(color='silver', Direction=135,
Strength=16)")
$txtstream.WriteLine("}")
$txtstream.WriteLine("th")
$txtstream.WriteLine("{")
$txtstream.WriteLine("    BORDER-RIGHT: #999999 3px solid;")
$txtstream.WriteLine("    PADDING-RIGHT: 6px;")
$txtstream.WriteLine("    PADDING-LEFT: 6px;")
$txtstream.WriteLine("    FONT-WEIGHT: Bold;")
$txtstream.WriteLine("    FONT-SIZE: 14px;")
$txtstream.WriteLine("    PADDING-BOTTOM: 6px;")
$txtstream.WriteLine("    COLOR: darkred;")
$txtstream.WriteLine("    LINE-HEIGHT: 14px;")
$txtstream.WriteLine("    PADDING-TOP: 6px;")
$txtstream.WriteLine("    BORDER-BOTTOM: #999 1px solid;")
$txtstream.WriteLine("    BACKGROUND-COLOR: #eeeeee;")
$txtstream.WriteLine("    FONT-FAMILY: Cambria, serif;")
$txtstream.WriteLine("    FONT-SIZE: 12px;")
$txtstream.WriteLine("    text-align: left;")
$txtstream.WriteLine("    white-Space: nowrap='nowrap';")
$txtstream.WriteLine("}")
$txtstream.WriteLine(".th")
$txtstream.WriteLine("{")
$txtstream.WriteLine("    BORDER-RIGHT: #999999 2px solid;")
$txtstream.WriteLine("    PADDING-RIGHT: 6px;")
$txtstream.WriteLine("    PADDING-LEFT: 6px;")
$txtstream.WriteLine("    FONT-WEIGHT: Bold;")
$txtstream.WriteLine("    PADDING-BOTTOM: 6px;")
$txtstream.WriteLine("    COLOR: black;")
$txtstream.WriteLine("    PADDING-TOP: 6px;")
$txtstream.WriteLine("    BORDER-BOTTOM: #999 2px solid;")
$txtstream.WriteLine("    BACKGROUND-COLOR: #eeeeee;")
$txtstream.WriteLine("    FONT-FAMILY: Cambria, serif;")
$txtstream.WriteLine("    FONT-SIZE: 10px;")
$txtstream.WriteLine("    text-align: right;")
$txtstream.WriteLine("    white-Space: nowrap='nowrap';")
$txtstream.WriteLine("}")
$txtstream.WriteLine("td")
$txtstream.WriteLine("{")
$txtstream.WriteLine("    BORDER-RIGHT: #999999 3px solid;")
$txtstream.WriteLine("    PADDING-RIGHT: 6px;")
$txtstream.WriteLine("    PADDING-LEFT: 6px;")
$txtstream.WriteLine("    FONT-WEIGHT: Normal;")
$txtstream.WriteLine("    PADDING-BOTTOM: 6px;")
$txtstream.WriteLine("    COLOR: navy;")
$txtstream.WriteLine("    LINE-HEIGHT: 14px;")
```

```
$txtstream.WriteLine("   PADDING-TOP: 6px;")
$txtstream.WriteLine("   BORDER-BOTTOM: #999 1px solid;")
$txtstream.WriteLine("   BACKGROUND-COLOR: #eeeeee;")
$txtstream.WriteLine("   FONT-FAMILY: Cambria, serif;")
$txtstream.WriteLine("   FONT-SIZE: 12px;")
$txtstream.WriteLine("   text-align: left;")
$txtstream.WriteLine("   white-Space: nowrap='nowrap';")
$txtstream.WriteLine("}")
$txtstream.WriteLine("div")
$txtstream.WriteLine("{")
$txtstream.WriteLine("   BORDER-RIGHT: #999999 3px solid;")
$txtstream.WriteLine("   PADDING-RIGHT: 6px;")
$txtstream.WriteLine("   PADDING-LEFT: 6px;")
$txtstream.WriteLine("   FONT-WEIGHT: Normal;")
$txtstream.WriteLine("   PADDING-BOTTOM: 6px;")
$txtstream.WriteLine("   COLOR: white;")
$txtstream.WriteLine("   PADDING-TOP: 6px;")
$txtstream.WriteLine("   BORDER-BOTTOM: #999 1px solid;")
$txtstream.WriteLine("   BACKGROUND-COLOR: navy;")
$txtstream.WriteLine("   FONT-FAMILY: Cambria, serif;")
$txtstream.WriteLine("   FONT-SIZE: 10px;")
$txtstream.WriteLine("   text-align: left;")
$txtstream.WriteLine("   white-Space: nowrap='nowrap';")
$txtstream.WriteLine("}")
$txtstream.WriteLine("span")
$txtstream.WriteLine("{")
$txtstream.WriteLine("   BORDER-RIGHT: #999999 3px solid;")
$txtstream.WriteLine("   PADDING-RIGHT: 3px;")
$txtstream.WriteLine("   PADDING-LEFT: 3px;")
$txtstream.WriteLine("   FONT-WEIGHT: Normal;")
$txtstream.WriteLine("   PADDING-BOTTOM: 3px;")
$txtstream.WriteLine("   COLOR: white;")
$txtstream.WriteLine("   PADDING-TOP: 3px;")
$txtstream.WriteLine("   BORDER-BOTTOM: #999 1px solid;")
$txtstream.WriteLine("   BACKGROUND-COLOR: navy;")
$txtstream.WriteLine("   FONT-FAMILY: Cambria, serif;")
$txtstream.WriteLine("   FONT-SIZE: 10px;")
$txtstream.WriteLine("   text-align: left;")
$txtstream.WriteLine("   white-Space: nowrap='nowrap';")
$txtstream.WriteLine("   display: inline-block;")
$txtstream.WriteLine("   width: 100%;")
$txtstream.WriteLine("}")
$txtstream.WriteLine("textarea")
$txtstream.WriteLine("{")
$txtstream.WriteLine("   BORDER-RIGHT: #999999 3px solid;")
$txtstream.WriteLine("   PADDING-RIGHT: 3px;")
$txtstream.WriteLine("   PADDING-LEFT: 3px;")
$txtstream.WriteLine("   FONT-WEIGHT: Normal;")
$txtstream.WriteLine("   PADDING-BOTTOM: 3px;")
$txtstream.WriteLine("   COLOR: white;")
```

```
$txtstream.WriteLine("    PADDING-TOP: 3px;")
$txtstream.WriteLine("    BORDER-BOTTOM: #999 1px solid;")
$txtstream.WriteLine("    BACKGROUND-COLOR: navy;")
$txtstream.WriteLine("    FONT-FAMILY:  Cambria, serif;")
$txtstream.WriteLine("    FONT-SIZE: 10px;")
$txtstream.WriteLine("    text-align: left;")
$txtstream.WriteLine("    white-Space: nowrap='nowrap';")
$txtstream.WriteLine("    width: 100%;")
$txtstream.WriteLine("}")
$txtstream.WriteLine("select")
$txtstream.WriteLine("{")
$txtstream.WriteLine("    BORDER-RIGHT: #999999 3px solid;")
$txtstream.WriteLine("    PADDING-RIGHT: 6px;")
$txtstream.WriteLine("    PADDING-LEFT: 6px;")
$txtstream.WriteLine("    FONT-WEIGHT: Normal;")
$txtstream.WriteLine("    PADDING-BOTTOM: 6px;")
$txtstream.WriteLine("    COLOR: white;")
$txtstream.WriteLine("    PADDING-TOP: 6px;")
$txtstream.WriteLine("    BORDER-BOTTOM: #999 1px solid;")
$txtstream.WriteLine("    BACKGROUND-COLOR: navy;")
$txtstream.WriteLine("    FONT-FAMILY:  Cambria, serif;")
$txtstream.WriteLine("    FONT-SIZE: 10px;")
$txtstream.WriteLine("    text-align: left;")
$txtstream.WriteLine("    white-Space: nowrap='nowrap';")
$txtstream.WriteLine("    width: 100%;")
$txtstream.WriteLine("}")
$txtstream.WriteLine("input")
$txtstream.WriteLine("{")
$txtstream.WriteLine("    BORDER-RIGHT: #999999 3px solid;")
$txtstream.WriteLine("    PADDING-RIGHT: 3px;")
$txtstream.WriteLine("    PADDING-LEFT: 3px;")
$txtstream.WriteLine("    FONT-WEIGHT: Bold;")
$txtstream.WriteLine("    PADDING-BOTTOM: 3px;")
$txtstream.WriteLine("    COLOR: white;")
$txtstream.WriteLine("    PADDING-TOP: 3px;")
$txtstream.WriteLine("    BORDER-BOTTOM: #999 1px solid;")
$txtstream.WriteLine("    BACKGROUND-COLOR: navy;")
$txtstream.WriteLine("    FONT-FAMILY:  Cambria, serif;")
$txtstream.WriteLine("    FONT-SIZE: 12px;")
$txtstream.WriteLine("    text-align: left;")
$txtstream.WriteLine("    display: table-cell;")
$txtstream.WriteLine("    white-Space: nowrap='nowrap';")
$txtstream.WriteLine("    width: 100%;")
$txtstream.WriteLine("}")
$txtstream.WriteLine("h1 {")
$txtstream.WriteLine("color: antiquewhite;")
$txtstream.WriteLine("text-shadow: 1px 1px 1px black;")
$txtstream.WriteLine("padding: 3px;")
$txtstream.WriteLine("text-align: center;")
```

```
$txtstream.WriteLine("box-shadow: inset 2px 2px 5px rgba(0,0,0,0.5), inset -2px -
2px 5px rgba(255,255,255,0.5);")
$txtstream.WriteLine("}")
$txtstream.WriteLine("</style>")
```

www.ingramcontent.com/pod-product-compliance
Lightning Source LLC
Chambersburg PA
CBHW071550080326
40690CB00056B/1778